Do
Animals Fall
in Love?

We thank Ruben Holland from the Leipzig Zoo for his advice.

This edition first published in 2021 by Gecko Press
PO Box 9335, Wellington 6141, New Zealand
info@geckopress.com

English-language edition © Gecko Press Ltd 2021
Translation © Shelley Tanaka 2021

Originally published as *Das Liebesleben der Tiere* © 2017 Klett Kinderbuch
GmbH, Leipzig, Germany

The translation of this book was supported by a grant from the Goethe-Institut
which is funded by the German Ministry of Foreign Affairs.

Edited by Penelope Todd
Typesetting by Carolyn Lewis
Handwriting by Giselle Clarkson
Printed in China by Everbest Printing Co. Ltd, an accredited ISO 14001
& FSC-certified printer

ISBN hardback: 978-1-776572-91-5

For more curiously good books, visit geckopress.com

Katharina von der Gathen

Anke Kuhl

Do Animals Fall in Love?

GECKO PRESS

CONTENTS

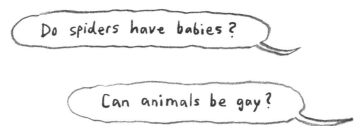

HOW DO ANIMALS DO IT?

Do animals have sex too?

How do elephants have sex?

And what about snakes?

These are the questions curious children ask when we talk with them about animals and sexual activity. In fact, at some point most people want to know how various animals create their offspring.

This is a book to read or browse through. It's a book about the animals that live nearby and in the remotest corners of our planet. It covers

• how they find and compete for mates,
• the unusual ways they have sex,
• how animal babies are conceived,
• and how they make their way into the world.

Over time, each species has developed its own strategies for these tasks. Looking at them through human eyes, we can only imagine what lies behind those individual actions. We can't always know, because we can't ask the animals themselves. But if we keep looking closely, we will learn many surprising truths.

On the following pages, you'll find the funny, the amazing, the weird and peculiar, the familiar and the strange—glimpses and examples of the infinite ways animals love each other.

One thing is very clear. Anything and everything is possible!

I LIKE YOU!

THE ART OF SEDUCTION

IT'S SHOWTIME!

During courtship, animals have to work hard to find a suitable partner. It's all about producing offspring and passing on their unique characteristics. In most cases, the females get to be choosy, while the males have to make an impression. So they prance, dance, sing and fight to show off what they can do. It takes a lot of energy to outdo the competition. But once a choice has been made, the actual mating often takes just a few moments.

LOOK AT ME

FLAMBOYANT
Birds of Paradise

First, get their attention. In New Guinea, the many different birds of paradise turn mating into fireworks. The males, who already fly about in glorious iridescent hues, transform themselves further to woo the females. They might puff up their feathers and perform dance routines or flare their wings and necks to produce face-like patterns on their bodies. Some look like erupting volcanoes, perched on their branches. Others spread and flaunt their feather fans.

The males of some species gather in a special display area. Beforehand, they'll often clean and tidy it, carrying away loose sticks and stray leaves until the courtship arena is spotless. Each bird has its own place, depending on its rank. The prime spots are reserved for the oldest and most beautiful males. The young birds can join in, of course, but they're too inexperienced to impress many of the females.

When the hopping and singing begin, feathers flutter everywhere. From above, or off to one side, the females watch

the spectacle, and each one makes her choice. Usually, they'll pick the male with the best combination of song, feathers and dance. He is then allowed to fertilize the female's eggs.

MAGNIFICENT
Red Deer

Every year, a miraculous structure of bone, skin and hair grows on a male deer's head: the antlers. The male deer (stag) proudly bears this crown through the forest, roaring loudly to let everyone

crown

trez tines

bez tines
brow tines

Royal stag: 12 tines (points)

15

know: I'm gorgeous. I'm strong. I'm ready to mate! The more impressive the antlers, the better his chances with the does (female deer). Large antlers can also be used as a weapon in duels with other males. Towards the end of the winter, this beautiful headgear simply falls off, to be left dangling from a tree or lying on the forest floor. It doesn't matter. In summer he'll grow a new set of antlers even bigger and more impressive than the old ones.

FLASHY

Fireflies

If you've ever seen fireflies on a balmy summer night, you already know how fascinating these neon-green dancing points of light can be when there are hundreds in the air at a time. Fireflies don't do this just for fun. They have something important in mind. They're looking for a mate. Fireflies aren't flies at all. They're black and brown beetles that crawl on the ground by day, but in the dark shine with a magical beauty. Mostly only the males can fly, while the females watch the light show from the ground and flash energetically back. Each type of firefly communicates through its own light version of Morse code, which differs from others in brightness and rhythm.

But watch out! The females of a certain type of North American firefly know foreign languages and can play a nasty trick, imitating the flash patterns of another species. In that case the foreign male can't expect an act of love. More likely he'll end up as dinner—between the mouthparts of a greedy imposter.

FAN DANCE
Peafowl

Peacocks have wonderfully long tail feathers that can form impressive-looking fans. The male birds gather in a mating area to show off their beauty to the females. They strut in circles, rustling their fans to display the dazzling rainbow. The shinier the feathers, the more iridescent the eyes on a peacock's tail and the more symmetrical their pattern, the greater his chances with the peahens. The chicks that hatch from the eggs he fertilizes will be more robust, too, and the males will have their own impressive tail fans when they grow up.

CREATIVE
Pufferfish

The male white-spotted pufferfish shows himself to be a true artist when he prepares a nest for a female. Over several days, he swims close to the seabed, carving grooves in the sand with his fins to create a fascinating mandala pattern on the ocean floor.

A female swimming by will recognize at once that this is a good place to spawn and lay her eggs. She swims into the middle of the circle where her artistic mate gently bites her cheek, which begins the mating ritual.

17

For everyday

For courtship

ALL PUFFED UP
Frigatebirds

Party balloons have nothing on the bright red balloons that male frigatebirds inflate during courtship. The seabirds throw themselves ashore and take up position in the nesting area. They beat their wings, rattle their bills and inflate their bright red throat sacs into oversized balloons while females fly overhead. Clearly the female frigatebirds find these fat red balls irresistible. However, once two birds have paired up, this display of male beauty quickly shrinks away. As soon as the female becomes pregnant, a shrivelled sac on the neck is all that remains of the plump balloon.

ARTISTIC
Bowerbirds

What an effort! Male bowerbirds take months building their love nests—decorating, cleaning and beautifying them to attract a female. Because they themselves are plain and can't show off spectacular plumage or put on an eye-catching dance performance, they have to impress with their artistic talent. Look, they say, I have the nicest apartment of all!

After fertilization, however, the painstaking constructions play no further role. The females lay their eggs in normal nests high up in the trees.

Each bowerbird has its own advertising strategy.

18

MacGregor's bowerbird builds a kind of tower from branches, which stands like a Christmas tree in a moss-draped circle. The area around it is thoroughly cleared of branches and litter. Glittering threads of animal hair or caterpillar poo decorate the lower branches of the tower like festive Christmas decorations.

The **satin bowerbird** loves everything blue. He collects berries, blossoms, feathers and bits of blue plastic or glass to attract females to his bower. The bower itself is a corridor of artistically arranged branches, and sometimes the walls are even painted with berry juice or charcoal.

As the name suggests, the **great grey bowerbird** prefers the more muted shades. He collects stones, shards of bone, snail shells, pieces of snakeskin or butterfly wing, bits of plastic, bottle caps and mosses to make the area around his nest as interesting as possible. He is also quite competitive and may even destroy another male's construction.

Five-star room!

★ ★ ★

DANCE WITH ME

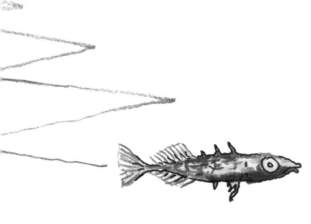

Peacock Spiders

Dark googly eyes, a rainbow tail-flap, striped hairy legs—the male of this species of jumping spider can leave quite an impression. But good looks alone are not enough. He also needs to be such a good dancer that discerning females will stop for a moment to watch. The hind legs wave and shake, the front legs tap out a rhythm, and he scuttles back and forth like ground crew guiding a plane on a runway.

ZIGZAG
Sticklebacks

The male of this small fish species goes to a lot of effort in the mating season. First, he prepares the nest for eggs, lining it with algae and plants. Then he signals for attention with his bright red belly. Finally, he shows off his dance-swimming, demonstrating with his fast zigzag style that he's physically fit and agile. He darts back and forth in front of the stickleback female, leading her to his love nest where she can empty her egg-filled belly. The male now gets to fertilize the eggs, making the dance performance worth it.

Peacock spiders, lifesize

Well, well...

Male

Female

Great Crested Grebes

You can observe water ballet of the highest order with the great crested grebe. The males and females meet on the water and perform the most elegant dance routine, as if they've been rehearsing for months. Again and again they swim towards each other, stretching their necks high and shaking their heads in unison, touching bellies and beaks. Eventually they dive together, picking up lake-weed from the bottom and holding it up to their partner's beak as if to say, Look! This will make a nice nest for our little grebes!

Seahorses

Before they get down to it, a seahorse couple does a seductive mating dance that lasts for many hours. Male and female swim artfully around each other, pirouetting and interlacing tails over and over again. The skins of some species also change to the most dazzling pigments. For the grand finale, the seahorses press their bellies together so the female can deliver many hundreds of eggs into the male's brood pouch.

IN SYNC
Flamingos

For flamingos, winning a female is no solo performance. The males gather for a group dance. As soon as one bird takes the first steps and stretches out his neck, the other males follow suit. All together now: five steps to the left, five steps to the right, beat your wings, head to the left, head to the right, step, sway, turn and start again...

SOMETHING'S IN THE AIR

EACH TO THEIR OWN
Dromedaries (Arabian Camels)

For months the male dromedary has one thing in mind: when can I finally get going? He'll sniff at the rear ends of females again and again, checking for the smell of the special hormones that form in the mating season. Sometimes he'll rudely kick and shove the female until she pees. Then he can tell if it's time, not only by the smell of her hindquarters, but also by the taste of her pee.

And he sends out signals of his own. He spreads his dung around the place by swishing his tail. Any ready-to-mate females evidently find the smell exciting!

SWISH SWISH

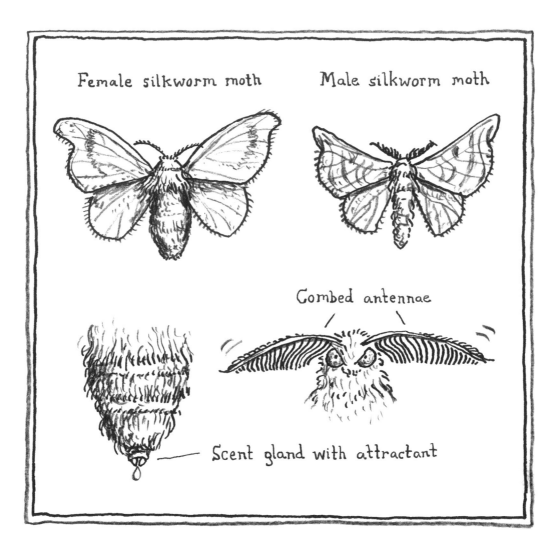

Female silkworm moth

Male silkworm moth

Combed antennae

Scent gland with attractant

SENSITIVE
Silkworm Moths

It's not always the male who takes the first step in a love match. In some cases the female attracts a mate, say with a special perfume that the male can sense. This is how it is with the silkworm moth. These are inconspicuous moths whose females can send out a special sex scent. Using antennae that spread out like combs from his head, a male can sense the tiniest amount of this female attractant from an enormous distance—like smelling your dad cook up a delicious spaghetti sauce while you're still sitting at your friend's house. As soon as a male has sniffed out a partner, he'll make his way to her through rain, sleet or snow.

IRRESISTIBLE
Musk Deer

Extra-fine antennae aren't always needed to detect sex hormones. Young male musk deer attract females with a strong-smelling liquid produced by a gland on their lower abdomen. When they're ready to mate, they smear this liquid on tree bark and shrubs throughout the forest, marking their territory. The smell is so intense that females find it irresistible. Humans can smell it even when it's highly diluted. (Musk is the ingredient that gives many perfumes that certain sexy something.)

★ ★ ★

LOVE SONGS

GREATEST HITS
Humpback Whales

Big male humpback whales sing, squeak, moan and grunt, perhaps to attract female whales, who are often swimming many miles away. The males all sing the same song, for up to days at a time, sometimes adding new variations. When the song becomes too complex, they start up a new one that soon spreads through the whole humpback population.

Swimming through the deep blue sea, lovely lady, come to me!

SINGING SENSATION
Nightingales

This little bird looks unremarkable. But if the nightingale does one thing well, it's singing. As the name suggests, by night the males sing, whistle and warble for hours to please the female nightingales. Their songs are unique in the bird world. A male can perform more than 180 different verses, each one richly varied and beautiful. The female listens carefully because the more complex and energetic the singing, the healthier and stronger the male, which should make him a good father for the upcoming spring brood.

SIREN SONG
Gibbons

These apes perform impressive duets. Their whooping siren calls can pierce the densest jungle over long distances. Once a pair of gibbons has found one another, they'll attune their yelps and chirps into long successive stanzas. The strength and harmony of a couple's song is a sign of how strongly bonded they are.

BIG BUZZ
Toadfish

Silent as a fish? You must be kidding. Some fish make amazing sounds underwater. They growl, buzz, drone, grunt, hum and croak. The toadfish is particularly expressive. To attract a female, he buzzes his most beautiful love song. He drones and hums for hours at a time, and if many males are doing it at once, the sound can carry beyond the water and even make boat hulls shudder. The sound is like a cell phone vibrating and is created when the toadfish's muscles vibrate his swim bladder.

Normally, a female can't hear the male's hum very well. When she has eggs ready to be fertilized, her inner ear changes, and only then can she clearly sense the love song and be drawn to it. Meanwhile, the male has prepared a nest and waits there, droning away until the future mother of his fish children finally joins him for mating.

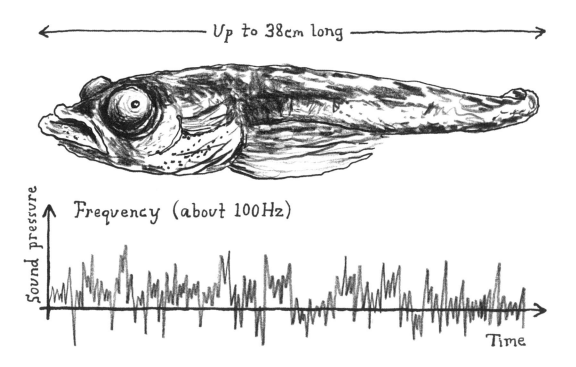

Up to 38cm long

Frequency (about 100 Hz)

Sound pressure

Time

WIND INSTRUMENT

Frogs

When other animals go to sleep on summer nights, frogs really get going. To attract the attention of females, the males croak with all their might, creating a chorus of different notes and tones. Frogs use vocal sacs as instruments; these protrude on each side of their jaw or form a big balloon under the mouth. The bigger the sac, the louder the call.

Single air sac

Double air sacs

★ ★ ★

CLASH OF THE RIVALS

BIG BANG
Musk oxen

Musk oxen bulls aren't especially subtle. They gallop towards each other with lowered heads...until they crash together with a loud bang. They do this over and over until one of them is so weak he has to walk away.

Luckily, musk oxen are hardheaded. They have a wide, horned plate on their forehead just for these fights. The winner gets to mate with the females—until a new competitor turns up with a tougher forehead.

IN THE RING
Kangaroos

When two male kangaroos fight over a female during the mating season, it's a real boxing match. They bounce around, hitting, shoving and wrestling. A kick from those strong hind legs can seriously injure an opponent.

PUSHED AROUND
Stag Beetles

No, those aren't antlers on a male stag beetle's head. They're upper jaws, which he uses to compete for females. Two competitors strive to push or pry each other off a branch. Whoever remains has won the right to be the first to mate with a female.

TOUGH STUFF
Zebras

Zebras aren't squeamish. When it's a matter of winning a female, the stallions whack their heads and necks at each other, bite each other's forelegs and kick out with their hind legs. It can be an epic battle with a gory ending.

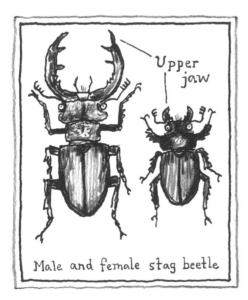

Upper jaw

Male and female stag beetle

HEADACHE
Red Deer

When he's ready to mate, a male red deer goes looking for a fight. If there's no opponent around, he'll let off steam by attacking trees or the forest floor with his antlers. When two rivals do come together, they fight to the point of exhaustion. They run at each other, hooking antlers, pushing and shoving until one gives up. At the end of the rutting (mating) season, the stags are completely tuckered out. Some have lost so much weight they can barely stand.

Very rarely, the stags' antlers get hopelessly entangled and neither can get away. In the worst case, they die together, antler to antler.

BEATEN UP
Brown Hares

A female brown hare sometimes vigorously beats up the male if he's chasing her around too much during the mating season. She might also be testing to see how strong he is before she'll accept him as the father of her future children.

You're the best, the loveliest and the smartest...

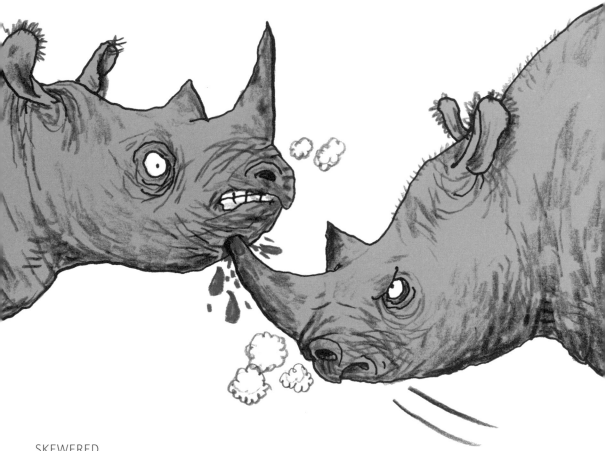

SKEWERED
Rhinoceroses

Rhinos use their imposing horns (some species come with two horns—a double threat) as combat devices, especially during mating season. When two bulls run into each other, there can be a bloody conflict. The opponents approach each other hesitantly at first, heads lowered, swinging their horns from side to side and pawing with their hind feet in a threatening way. Then suddenly they rush at each another. In the worst case, the fight ends fatally for one of them because of gaping wounds from their opponent's horns.

Sometimes the threat is as far as it goes. Being near-sighted, bulls have to recognize by smell who they're facing. When they stop short of colliding and turn away, it's because they're satisfied that their actions have made the right impression.

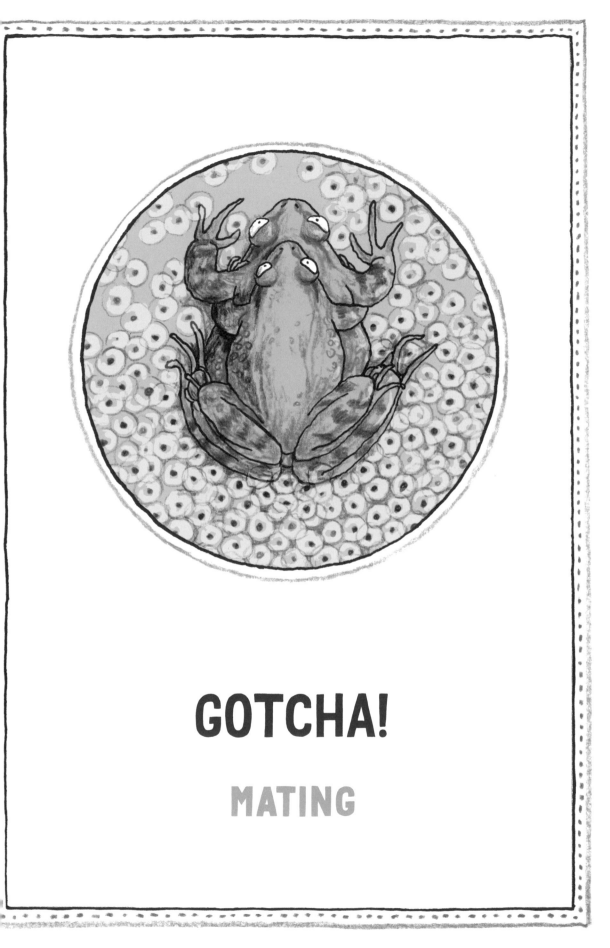

GOTCHA!

MATING

Sex? It's pretty quick for me these days...

Almost all living beings have sex. It's the best way for many species to go on existing and evolving. For most animals, it's important to pair up when they are fertile and can produce offspring.

Different animal species have sex in different ways and different places. These can even vary within a species. However, the principle is almost always the same. Somehow, sperm cells from a male and egg cells from a female find each other and merge to form a new and unique life.

 **FISH** reproduce in different ways. With most species of fish, females and males simply deposit eggs and sperm into the water at the same time (spawning). The eggs of the female are fertilized as they float about. They mature in protected spaces between aquatic plants until the small fish larvae are ready to hatch. Other fish species fertilize eggs while they're still in the female's body. The male fish has a special fin like a penis that directs the sperm into the female. The fish larvae hatch inside the mother and then come out of her body as baby fish.

 **MAMMALS** are named this because the offspring drink milk from their mothers' mammory glands. Fertilization takes place when sperm flows from the male's stiff penis through the vagina of the mother to the egg cells. For most mammals, the baby grows inside the uterus until it finally enters the world through the vagina. Sometimes there are several offspring.

Most female **INSECTS** lay their eggs after being fertilized by a male. Some males have something like a penis or specialized arms to deliver the sperm. Others simply deposit a "package" of sperm on the ground to be picked up by a female through her cloaca (genital opening).

BIRDS' eggs are fertilized in the body of the female. Most bird species press their cloacas together for a few seconds. The sperm flows from the male in through the female's opening to the egg cells. The eggs are surrounded by a stable chalky shell inside the female, then laid in a nest and incubated.

AMPHIBIANS such as frogs and salamanders live both in water and on land. The eggs are mostly fertilized in the water, where the developing creatures, the larvae, will hatch. Often the male clings to the female so firmly that he notices the moment the eggs emerge and can quickly spray them with his sperm.

A male **SPIDER** has special syringe-like appendages (pedipalps) on the "head" part of his body (the cephalothorax), which he uses to inject sperm. The female lets the pedipalps slip into her genital opening so the mate gets rid of his sperm as quickly as possible. Females then often complete the sex act by literally having their partner for dinner!

In the case of **REPTILES** like snakes and lizards, a male fertilizes the female's eggs using a penis-like organ that works as a chute that funnels sperm into the female's cloaca. In most cases, she then lays her eggs on land to hatch in warm sandy soil. Sometimes, though, they remain in the body, so the offspring can be hatched inside the mother and born as baby reptiles.

MANY ROADS LEAD TO THE EGG

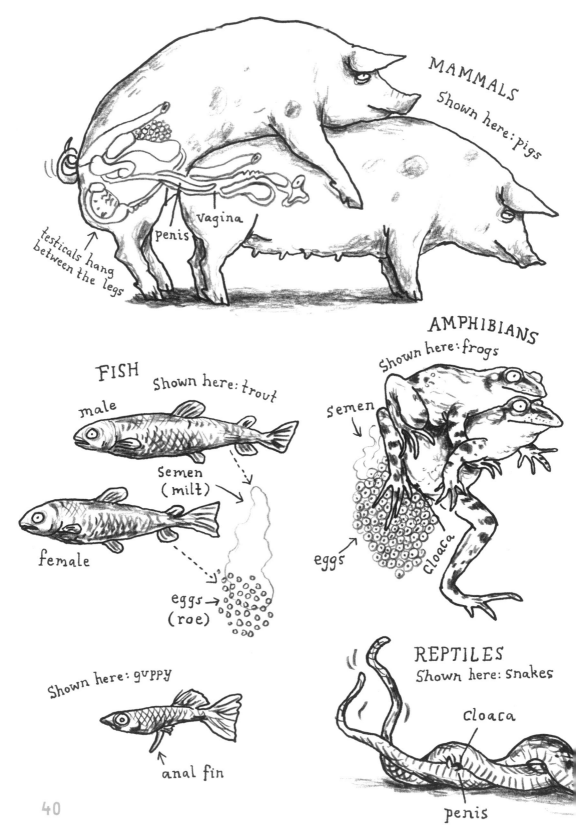

MAMMALS
Shown here: pigs

testicals hang between the legs

penis

Vagina

FISH
Shown here: trout

male

Semen (milt)

female

eggs (roe)

Shown here: guppy

anal fin

AMPHIBIANS
Shown here: frogs

semen

eggs

Cloaca

REPTILES
Shown here: snakes

Cloaca

penis

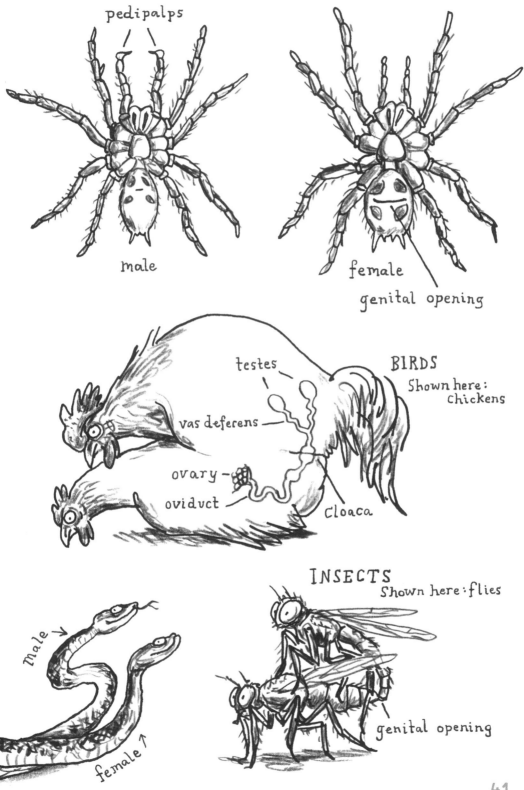

SPIDERS Shown here: tarantula

pedipalps

male

female
genital opening

BIRDS
Shown here:
chickens

testes

vas deferens

ovary

oviduct

Cloaca

INSECTS
Shown here: flies

male

female

genital opening

ONCE IN A LIFETIME? ANIMALS THAT SELDOM HAVE SEX

FRUGAL

Ants

A queen ant can produce an entire colony with a single sex act. To prepare for this event, she and all the other mature adult females and males grow wings. One day they all gather for the so-called nuptial flight, to mate in a cloud of buzzing black dots. If the mating is successful, each queen breaks off her own wings and finds a protected spot to deposit her eggs, since she has collected enough

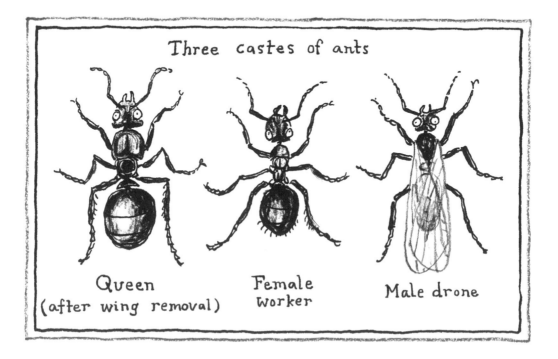

Three castes of ants

Queen
(after wing removal)

Female
worker

Male drone

sperm to start her own ant colony. The males die not long after mating since they're no longer needed.

The ant queen can store the collected sperm in her abdomen for the rest of her life and fertilize millions of eggs. As soon as enough female worker ants have hatched, the queen's only job is to produce more eggs and decide whether or not they'll be fertilized from the sperm supply. All the other necessary work, such as foraging for food, nesting and raising the offspring, is done by the female worker ants.

Male drones develop only from unfertilized eggs. They don't have much to do in the queen's colony and can only serve as sperm donors in the next nuptial flight.

LUSTLESS
Giant Pandas

Pandas hardly ever feel desire. Least of all for sex. And so they spend most of their lives sitting around chewing. And chewing. And chewing...on one bamboo leaf after another. For up to 16 hours a day. This is exhausting and generally keeps them busy enough. But for about two days a year, female pandas let the males know that they just might be interested in sex. That's not often. Along with human impacts, this may be a reason why there are so few pandas in the world.

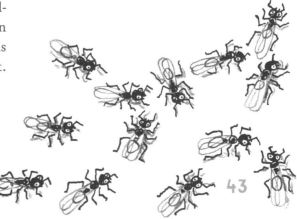

ONE-OFF
Bees

Male honeybees, called drones, have fun just once in their lives (though no one knows for sure if they'd describe their nuptial flight with the queen bee as "fun"). During mid-air sex, the drone shoots his sperm explosively, all at once, into the queen bee's reproductive organs. The drone's penis usually rips off inside the body of the queen, and he falls to his death. He has fulfilled the sole purpose of his existence, which is to ensure the survival of the honeybee colony—even if it costs him his life.

EVERY 17 YEARS
Cicadas

Male and female cicadas rarely have anything to do with each other. For several years—up to 17 in the case of one American species—the small larvae crawl around deep down in the forest floor. Until one night, as if alerted by a secret signal, they come to the surface with one goal in mind. Cicada sex! They crawl out of the ground by the billions to go through a spectacular transformation. They cling to the surrounding trees, leaves, branches and twigs and their carapaces suddenly explode. New winged creatures peel themselves out of the old shells.

The male insects soon begin to call to the cicada females with deafening chirps. They all have to hurry, because they have only a few weeks to live. They will die shortly after mating and laying eggs.

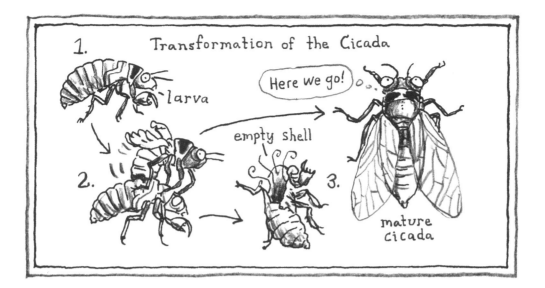

And it will be up to 17 years before their children are old enough to dig themselves out of the forest floor as crawling larvae and go searching for a mate for that single date.

PRIVATE

Eels

Scientists have only recently learned exactly how these snaky-bodied fish reproduce, and there are aspects of their life cycles that remain a mystery today. In many species, eels spend several years—or decades, even—in freshwater habitats, where they grow to adulthood.

When the time comes to breed, they make a journey that can be up to several thousand kilometers, returning to the marine area where they once hatched as tiny larvae from their eggs.

To mate, eels dive into the deepest depths of the sea, where they can be completely undisturbed and unobserved. Here, they lay eggs only once and then die soon after.

Not long after hatching, the new generation of eels migrates to the freshwater homelands of their parents. One day, they too will head back out to sea and dive down into the depths to mate.

OFTEN AND ALMOST ALWAYS

BAD FOR YOUR HEALTH

Antechinus

Once the male antechinus is sexually mature, there's no stopping him. Each year at around the same time, these small Australian marsupials get together. The males have one thing on their agenda: to mate with as many females as possible, for up to 14 hours at a time, over several days. They forget to eat or drink as they race through the forest in a hormone-driven frenzy. Before long, they're badly weakened by the stress of having so much sex. And yet they keep at it, looking for new females. After a few days, the male antechinuses are done in and die a painful death.

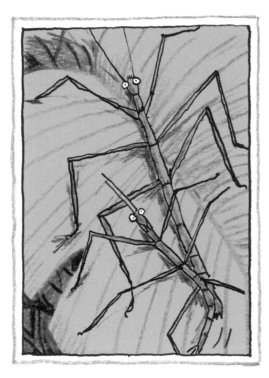

CONSTANT SEX
Stick insects

For up to 10 weeks at a time, the stick insect male clings to the much larger female to have sex with her. Again and again he inserts his penis into her and releases his sperm. While they're positioned this way, nothing can come between them, including another male. And the female doesn't seem to mind the extra weight on her back.

BE PREPARED!
Bonobos

Bonobos are a species of great ape. They live in family groups and are known to be extremely relaxed and peaceful. The most important reason for this is that they have a lot of sexual contact.

Bonobos communicate largely through physical affection, exchanging tongue kisses, caressing each other, having sex and experiencing pleasure in many different ways. When there's a dispute over food or after a fight, they relieve stress with the help of physical pleasure. It doesn't really seem to matter who the partner is. Everyone does it with everyone else. Old with young, male with male, female with female, male with female.

Much nicer than fighting!

All this sex helps to create strong social bonds. It doesn't usually take much time—about as long as it takes to count to five!

Sometimes the males dangle from branches and their stiff penises bang against each other. Or females rub their vulvas together until they experience sexual climax with loud squeals. This is how bonobos live calmly together with fewer conflicts than other apes.

24/7
Lions

When a lioness is "in heat" and ready to mate, she and the male lion have plenty of work ahead. Over several days they have sex up to 40 times a day, again and again. About every 15 minutes, the male climbs onto the female from behind and pushes briefly and vigorously.

It's quite exhausting, having so much sex! That's one reason a lion can't keep his position as chief inseminator of the pride for long. He only has a couple of years as protector and leader of his lionesses. After that, he's usually driven out by younger males and must make his way through life alone.

ALL TOGETHER NOW

Searching penis

Barnacles

In relation to their size, barnacles have the longest penises in the animal kingdom. And they need them too! For as soon as barnacles are past the larval stage, they settle down for the rest of their lives with the help of a particularly strong natural adhesive. You'll find colonies of barnacles stuck to rocks, stones or other animals such as whales. And when it comes to reproduction, you can see long tangles of penises criss-crossing as they reach out to the barnacle next door, each one feeling around for a fellow stationary partner.

ALL AT THE SAME TIME
Palolo Worms

When these sea creatures have sex, they all do it at the same time! On a certain night of the year, all the palolo worms living on coral reefs off the island of Samoa come together. During a particular phase of the moon, they meet on the ocean floor and unhitch the back sections of their bodies into the water. The sea teems with worm rumps floating to the surface, where they dissolve and release their precious cargo. On this night an incomparable orgy takes place in the coastal waters of Samoa, as eggs and sperm mix together in a fertile soup. Afterwards no one can say who has mated with whom.

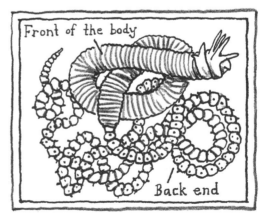

Front of the body

Back end

49

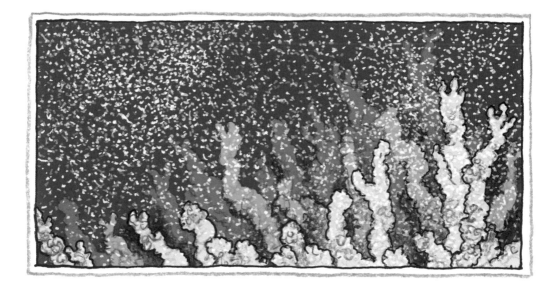

Meanwhile, the surviving fronts of the bodies remain undamaged deep down in the reef, and in a few days, their rear ends grow back. Next year this will happen again: everyone mating with everyone else, all together and at the same time.

UNDERWATER SNOWSTORM
Stony Corals

They look like strange bright plants growing on the seabed and rocks, and they provide habitat for fish and other ocean dwellers. But corals are also animals themselves. Like plants, these beautiful creations remain in one place for their entire lives. They slowly grow and solidify over time into a hard skeleton. The corals only drift freely in the water during the first days or weeks of their lives.

When the time comes for procreation, during one week of the year, the reef looks like a snowstorm on a clear winter's night. Established corals release billions of sperm and egg cells into the water at the same time to meet and form new coral babies. The tiny newbies are driven by currents and waves through the ocean until they find solid ground somewhere far away and establish themselves as new corals.

STACKED SEX
Slipper Shells

If you look at a slipper shell from below, it really does look like a tiny slipper. Even more interesting is that it's a type of hermaphrodite—it can grow first as one sex then change itself into another. How does this work? In piles! Slipper shells live and reproduce by stacking themselves on top of one another.

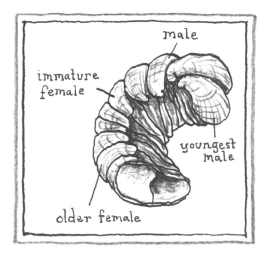

When a young male that's ready to mate comes across a female, he simply sets himself on top and hangs on, letting his penis dangle down. This young slipper shell snail remains the main inseminator until the next male comes along, when a wonderful transformation takes place. The male beneath gradually evolves into a female, and the "new guy" takes on the responsibility of fertilizing it. As many as 12 snails can stack on the sea floor this way, with males on top, females on the bottom and between them the snails that are gradually becoming females.

SPAGHETTI SEX

Snakes

Snakes having sex can look like a large plate of patterned spaghetti. The number of animals involved in the fun depends on the species. Sometimes there are only two, sometimes thousands. What a tangle it is when males and females curl around one another, rub together and rear up against each other! After some foreplay, two cloacas come together at last. The male pushes out his double penis and inserts one of them into the female's opening. Now the two are stuck fast. The female has nothing to worry about during mating because if she wants to leave, she just drags her partner along by his penis. Ouch! Good thing he has a spare.

EVERYONE WITH EVERYBODY

Ladybirds

Ladybirds love sex! As soon as they finish their winter hibernation, they start to mate. They're pretty persistent about it, too. One beetle sits on another for up to nine hours to fertilize the eggs in the female's body. After a couple of days, a new male ladybird may come along and pass on his seed packet, and then another male and another, again and again. Because everyone has sex with everyone else, disease-carrying parasites can also spread quickly. That doesn't seem to bother the beetles, though. They just keep going, because they've already done what's necessary to produce offspring.

My turn now!

SO NEAR AND SO FAR

REMOTE-CONTROLLED
Argonauts

Also called a paper nautilus, this is a kind of octopus living in the deep sea. The female has a mussel-shaped paper-thin egg case. The male is tiny in comparison and has no paper envelope, but he does have his own special feature—an extra-long penis-arm. When a female is ready to be fertilized, the male inserts his penis-arm into the female, where its semen packet bursts open to release its precious cargo. Then the penis-arm breaks off. Some females collect penis-arms like trophies, gathering them in the cavity of their mantle.

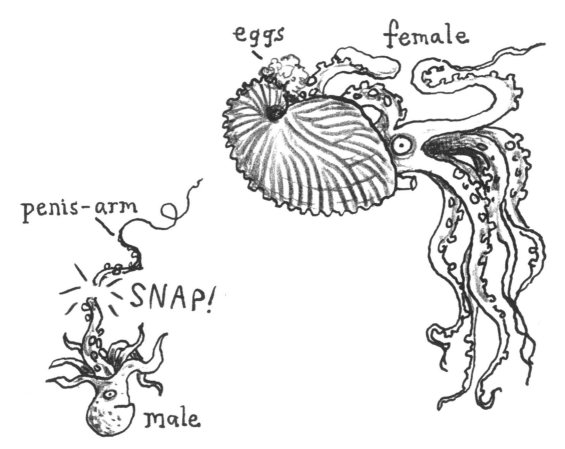

eggs

female

penis-arm

SNAP!

male

TOGETHER FOREVER
Anglerfish

In the infinite deep darkness of the ocean, it's not easy to find food or a companion. The female anglerfish has a kind of flashlight that shines directly in front of her mouth to help her find food. She also releases a scent to attract a male partner. Fortunately, he has an excellent sense of sight and smell. Otherwise the two would overlook each other, because the male is very tiny and featherlight. Sixty times smaller than the female, he floats inconspicuously through the ocean depths.

Once the two have found each other, the male bites onto the female's body so tightly that he eventually becomes a part of her. Most of his organs, such as the bowel, eyes and jaw, recede almost completely. Even their two bloodstreams become one. In this way, the male gets enough food and spends the rest of his life as a sperm donor for the female's eggs. They're bound together until death.

IN PASSING
Jellyfish

This is where things get slimy. They've been in our seas and oceans for millions of years. Jellyfish glide through the currents like magical parachute creatures, and they're made up of 95 percent water. They have no hearts or brains, but they do have nerve cells. Their sex organs shine as violet-pink rings in their transparent bodies. And some have sex only in passing. If a male meets a female jellyfish, they each release sperm or egg cells from their mouths into the water. However, this doesn't create baby jellyfish, but small larvae that swirl down through the sea. They attach themselves to rocky surfaces where they're transformed into polyps, small creatures a bit like anemones. Within a few weeks, the polyps change shape until each resembles a pile of cereal flakes. After a time, individual parts detach themselves from the polyps and swim away as a medusa (adult jellyfish). At last these life forms look the way you imagine jellyfish children should look!

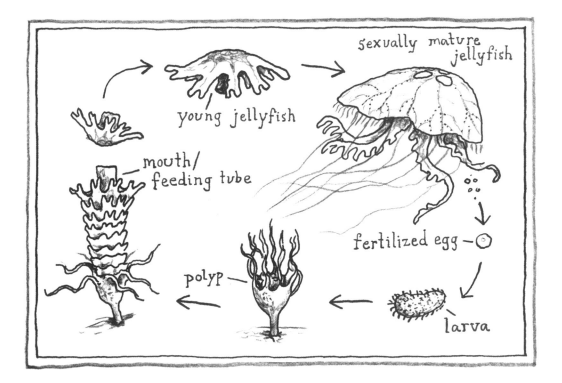

STUCK FAST

Dogs

Can a penis actually get stuck inside the partner during sex? With dogs, this is pretty normal. When the male climbs onto the female from behind, he pushes his stiffened penis into her vagina. Then he moves his rear end back and forth until the semen spurts out. But once he's finished it's not so easy to pull out, because his penis and the vaginal walls are so swollen. Neither of them can leave. It looks weird, but actually nature has set things up cleverly because this way the sperm stays inside the female thanks to the penis "cork."

Still connected, the male carefully turns around so they're bottom to bottom. Neither can go anywhere without the other. Luckily the dog's penis is very flexible. A backwards-bent penis could be pretty uncomfortable otherwise.

There's nothing left to do but wait. It can take up to half an hour for the swelling to subside so both animals are free to go.

1.

2.

3.

SO ATHLETIC

IN FLIGHT
Swifts

These little birds do everything in the air. They eat, drink, sleep and of course they also have sex. The latter is especially spectacular. The male flies to the female and settles on her back. While both plummet towards the earth with outstretched wings (they're too busy to beat their wings in flight), they hurriedly press their cloacas (sex openings) together. Quick as a flash, the male shoots out his seed—hopefully before they hit the ground.

BUNGEE SEX
Slugs

Slugs are hermaphrodites (both male and female at the same time), so they could actually fertilize themselves. Nonetheless they usually look for another slug of their own kind to mate with. Tiger slugs can hang upside down together for hours, each suspended from a tree by a slimy thread of mucus. Intertwined, they extend their blue-tinted penises, which grow out of their heads. The dangling penises lengthen gradually to about 20 cm. Only then do they wind together and the slugs fertilize each other's eggs.

←penises

Right and left and do-si-do...

DANCERS
Scorpions

Scorpions mate while dancing. They hold onto each other's pincers and, like a couple on the dance floor, caper forward, back, sideways, together (with the male leading).

At some point, the male deposits a pile of sticky sperm cells on the ground and guides the female to it. As soon as her genital opening is over it, the sperm can enter and fertilize her eggs. A scorpion doesn't need a penis.

SWORDPLAY
Flatworms

Actually, these don't look like worms at all. More like mini spaceships gliding through the water. Beautifully patterned and often shimmering, flatworms have developed a special way to reproduce. They duel with their penises. Like most worms, they are hermaphrodites. Both parents possess one or two penises as well as fertilizable eggs.

Their motto seems to be, "Anything but motherhood!" It's far simpler to deposit sperm for a few seconds than to deal with eggs. That seems to be the reason for their hour-long "fight."

The two of them rear and prance around one another, cleverly jousting and dodging until one finally thrusts its hard, pointy penis into the other's body. The one who stabs first becomes the father and says, "Off you go, and good luck with our kids!"

CARAVAN MARATHON
Echidnas

Before a female echidna (or spiny anteater) selects a mate, all applicants must prove themselves by following her in convoy. While she leads the parade, up to 10 males follow her. This can go on for weeks, over hill and dale, through bush and forest. It's quite exhausting for all participants!

And because she has to decide at some point, the female anteater eventually digs a nice crater around her, like a gladiatorial arena, where her suitors can fight for her and show off which is the best. She lies flat on the ground so that when the time comes, the chosen one can hoist himself up and finally get some action.

UPSIDE DOWN
Bats

When bats take a rest from flying around, they're known to hang upside down from the ceilings of caves. In many species, mating occurs in autumn before the females hibernate over the winter. A small bite on the neck wakes the coveted female up a bit and in her half-sleep she accepts the small stiff bat penis. She stores the sperm in her abdomen, while she goes on sleeping and chilling out. Only in the spring will she wake from hibernation and reactivate the sperm so that she can become pregnant and reproduce.

TRICKS AND DECEPTIONS

SAME-SEX TRICK
Mealworm Beetles

Even small male beetles have to defend themselves against competitors. Mealworm males use a special trick. They mate not only with female beetles around them, but also with other males who cross their path. If these males then mate with a female, they will first transfer the sperm of the same-sex beetle before they plant their own seed.

BY MOUTH
Cichlids

Cichlids are fish. In some species, after laying her eggs, the female quickly takes them into her mouth to protect them from enemies. That's where fertilization takes place, but only because the male cichlid uses a clever trick. He wears nice yellow spots on his rear end that look very similar to the female's eggs. The watchful female presumes she's forgotten a couple of eggs and opens her mouth to retrieve them. At this moment the male spurts out his seminal fluid, which mingles with the eggs in the female's mouth. His future children will remain safely in their mother's mouth until they're hatched.

SNEAKY
Giant Cuttlefish

Cuttlefish can camouflage themselves in the environment. Often you have to look very closely to recognize them. For example, they may be the same shade as the sandy seabed, or they may flicker like the algae they're hiding in.

Female giant cuttlefish are relatively small and inconspicuous, whereas males can be four times bigger. During the mating season, they impress the females with their constantly moving stripes, advertising themselves like neon signs. Only the biggest, strongest and most beautiful manage to hook one of the few females.

A smaller male can't compete with this show so he resorts to a trick. He "disguises" himself as a female by matching her appearance and narrower shape. Camouflaged like this, he can approach a mating couple without being recognized as a competitor. If all goes well, the interloper can deftly drop onto the female and mate with her at lightning speed. Often the larger, betrayed male doesn't even notice the deception and simply swims on with his partner. So you have to observe closely when these giants are mating. Not all the females slipping through the South Australian waters are what they seem.

GOSSAMER TRAILS
Silverfish

These often unloved housemates look like a primeval cross between fish and earwigs. Metallic and shiny, they whiz across bathroom floors and, before you know it, have vanished into the walls or under the carpets. The male silverfish has a special way of fertilizing the female. He weaves fine, gossamer threads over the floor and deposits his sperm capsule alongside. When the female detects the threads, she opens her ovipositor to take up the waiting sperm, and the fertilization of the silverfish eggs is done.

THE WAYS ANIMALS MATE

GIRAFFES

HOW OFTEN
Bonobos: all the time
Bedbugs: 200 times a day
Lions: up to 40 times a day
Doves: 7 times a day
Pandas: once a year
Eels: once in a lifetime

HOW LONG
Bonobos: 13 seconds
Rhinoceros: 1 hour
Mealworm beetles: 4 hours
Rattlesnakes: 22 hours
Prairie voles: 40 hours
Stick insects: 10 weeks

GIANT TORTOISE

← Groans amazingly loudly

DOLPHINS

Belly to belly

CAMELS

Male on his knees

TOADS

The toad has callused fingers – good for hanging on

HEDGEHOGS

That prickles!

ELEPHANTS

65

PENGUINS

Sitting position

Often face to face

GORILLAS

EARTHWORMS

Glued together

WHOA!

SOLO SEX!

Many animals also rub their sex organs with their hands, paws, fins, trunks or against objects and seem to get pleasure from it.

PLEASE DO NOT DISTURB!

BLACK BEAR

Masturbating →

INGENIOUS GENITALIA VULVAS, VAGINAS AND MORE

Most female mammals have a vulva. It includes the vaginal folds (labia), which form a cleft, with the clitoris at the top of the cleft. The clitoris is very sensitive and makes for nice feelings during sex. Between the labia a soft passage, the vagina, leads inside the body to the uterus. This is where the baby grows during a pregnancy. Other species, such as reptiles and amphibians, birds and insects, have a genital opening (cloaca) but no vulva.

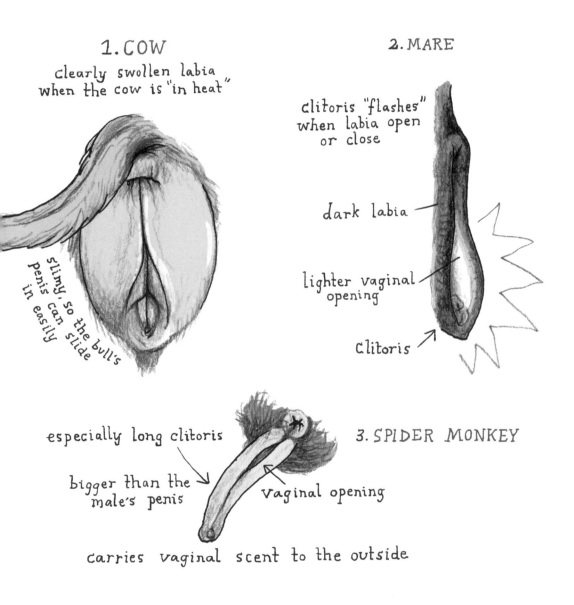

1. COW
clearly swollen labia
when the cow is "in heat"

slimy, so the bull's
penis can slide
in easily

2. MARE
clitoris "flashes"
when labia open
or close

dark labia —

lighter vaginal
opening

Clitoris ↗

especially long clitoris

bigger than the
male's penis ↘

vaginal opening

3. SPIDER MONKEY

carries vaginal scent to the outside

1.   2.   3.   4.   5.   6.   7.

4. BABOON

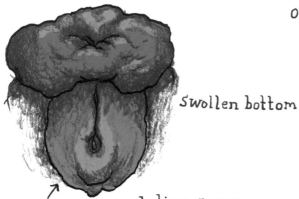

Swollen bottom

Swollen vaginal lips mean
"I'm ready to mate!"

5. KOALA
has two vaginas

ovary →

Vagina 1 →   ← Vagina 2

↑
vaginal entrance

6. HYENA

gigantic clitoris,
which can become stiff
like a penis
→

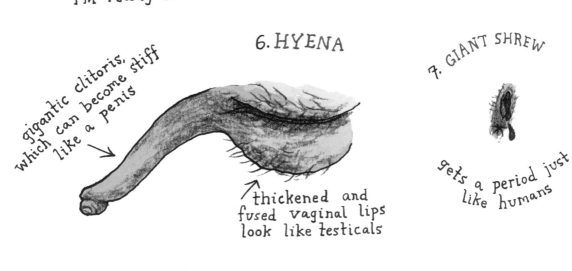

↑ thickened and
fused vaginal lips
look like testicals

7. GIANT SHREW

gets a period just
like humans

8. BLUE WHALE

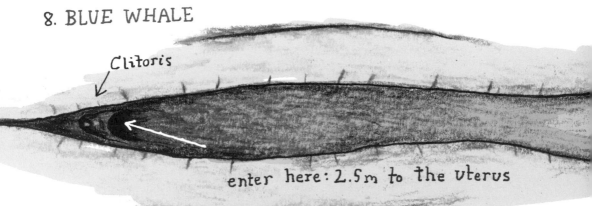

Clitoris

enter here: 2.5m to the uterus

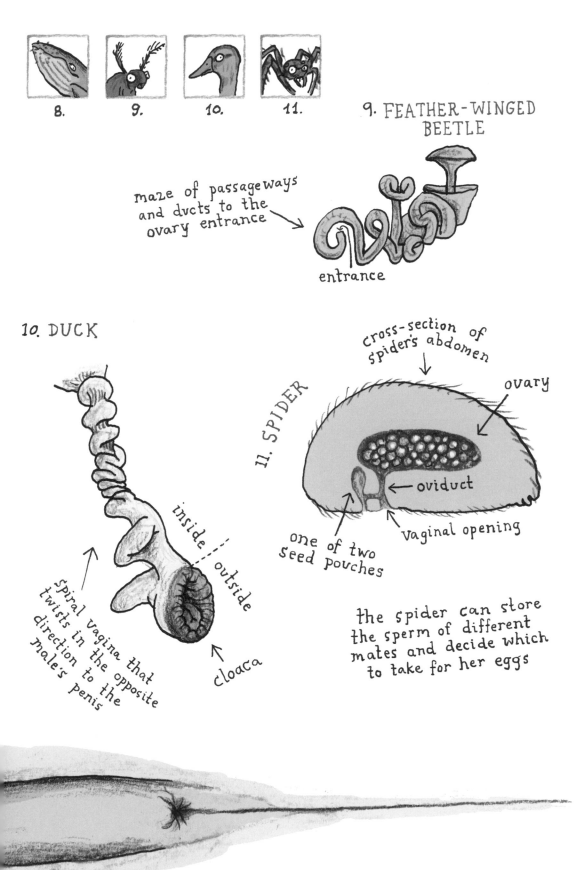

8.   9.   10.   11.

9. FEATHER-WINGED BEETLE

maze of passageways and ducts to the ovary entrance →

entrance

10. DUCK

11. SPIDER

cross-section of spider's abdomen

ovary

oviduct

Vaginal opening

one of two seed pouches

inside outside

spiral vagina that twists in the opposite direction to the male's penis

cloaca

the spider can store the sperm of different mates and decide which to take for her eggs

INGENIOUS GENITALIA PENISES

In the animal world, there's an incredible variety of penises. Males bring their sperm to females through their penises, ensuring that their genes are passed on. Probably conspicuous penises also impress the females and make them want to have sex. A specially shaped specimen can also trigger a nice feeling in the female (an orgasm).

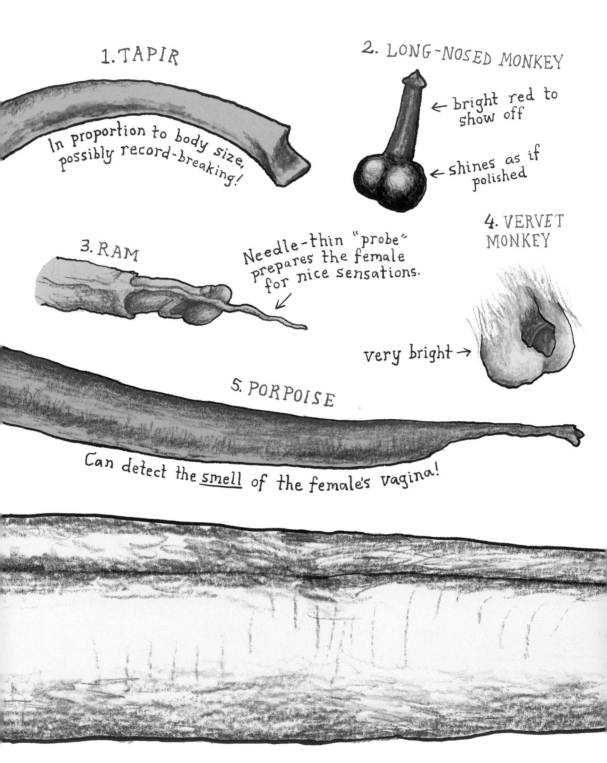

1. TAPIR

In proportion to body size, possibly record-breaking!

2. LONG-NOSED MONKEY

← bright red to show off

← shines as if polished

3. RAM

Needle-thin "probe" prepares the female for nice sensations.

4. VERVET MONKEY

very bright →

5. PORPOISE

Can detect the <u>smell</u> of the female's vagina!

1.   2.   3.   4.   5.   6.   7.

8.   9.   10.   11.   12.

6. HAMSTER

→ TINY PENIS
(Actual size)

7. BUFFALO WEAVER

UNIQUE AMONG BIRDS:

small rubbery false-penis for increased pleasure when rubbed against females during mating

8. ITALIAN TORTOISE

Looks like a little saucer →

9. SHARK

TWO-PRONGED!

the two "penises" are actually extensions of the pelvic fins

10. TOMCAT

barbed → OUCH!

11. LADYBIRDS

hooked penis →

12. BLUE WHALE HUGE! 3 m. long and as wide as a bucket

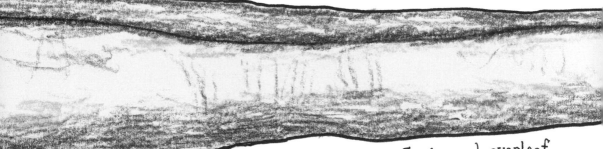

Continued overleaf

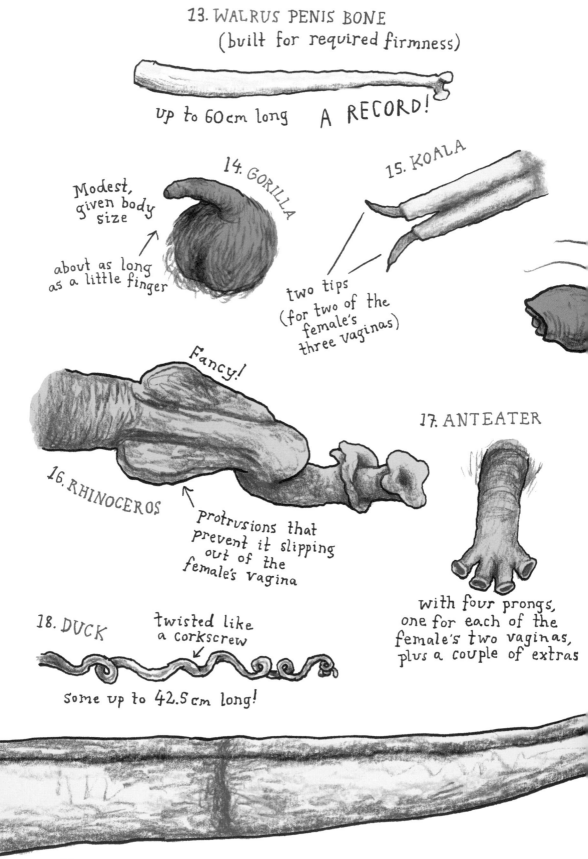

13. WALRUS PENIS BONE
(built for required firmness)

up to 60cm long   A RECORD!

14. GORILLA

Modest, given body size

about as long as a little finger

15. KOALA

two tips
(for two of the female's three vaginas)

Fancy!

16. RHINOCEROS

protrusions that prevent it slipping out of the female's vagina

17. ANTEATER

with four prongs, one for each of the female's two vaginas, plus a couple of extras

18. DUCK

twisted like a corkscrew

some up to 42.5cm long!

13.

14.

15.

16.

17.

18.

19.

20.

21.

19. ELEPHANT

very agile

also good for scratching
an itchy tummy

21. VESPER BAT

bent like a
window latch

covered with
shaggy hair

20. SNAKE

Double penis
with hooks so
it can't slip out

SPERM QUANTITY (per ejaculation or ejection)
Ram: 1 drop
Human: 1 tablespoon
Boar: 1 large glass
Right whale: 2 buckets

WHEN LOVE HURTS

DANGEROUS
Wasp Spiders

Black-and-yellow striped, she sits in her web and waits, motionless, for her partner. The female wasp spider is many times larger than the male, which means the male can deftly slip under the female for fertilization. Once there, belly to belly, he carefully tries to pass on his sperm. However, the interaction ends abruptly when the female grabs and eats the father of her spider children. Or when he runs away, leaving his mating organ stuck inside the female. Never again will he be able to have sex! He has escaped with his life, though, and ensured that the next generation will carry his genes.

BITE MARKS
Sharks

When it comes to sharks, there is no tenderness. On the contrary! The female shark has much to endure before she can look forward to offspring. The male harasses her and sinks his sharp teeth into her head or fins. Things can get pretty bloody. In the end, the male inserts

HELP!

one of his two penises into the female, and with a neat swoosh of seawater, his sperm is swept into her genital opening.

Many female sharks grow a thick layer of skin during puberty, which hopefully makes the attack more bearable.

SHORT AND PAINFUL
Cats

When you watch a little kitten play, it's hard to imagine him growing up to be brutal. There are many small spines and hooks on a cat's penis, which hurt the female quite a bit during sex. That's why the whole business only lasts a few seconds. It's thought that the pain triggers ovulation, which allows fertilization.

After mating, the female cat is not well disposed towards the male. With a few powerful paw swipes, she scares him off right after the act.

BRUTAL
Bedbugs

Male bedbugs should have to get a weapon license for their penis, and the females need combat training. During sex, the males don't ram their dagger-sharp sex organ into the female's genital opening, but rather, directly into her abdomen. This way the sperm gets into her body fluids and reaches the ovaries more quickly. The females often look badly battered, their body covered with puncture wounds. If there are many males around, it may all end with the violent sex death of the female bug.

VIOLENT
Ducks

Male ducks (drakes) can be extremely faithful, and after mating they often take loving care of the duck mothers, the nest building and the chicks. But when drakes are in the mood for sex, they can also be very violent. Several may rush at a female and try to mate with her at the same time. The female duck is brutally harassed, pursued underwater and mounted repeatedly in a great skirmish. Sometimes she's even drowned.

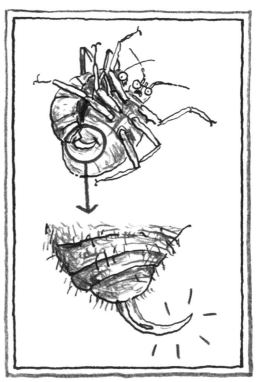

Love dart (highly magnified)

cross section

about 2mm

MOLLUSC WEAPONRY

Snails

Land snails are hermaphrodites, having both penis and vagina, and they produce both sperm and egg cells in their bodies. When it comes to sex, what starts as intimate snail lovemaking ends in a fight, because they have to work out which snail is going to provide the egg and which the sperm. It begins in a typically snail-like way. The snails rise veeeery slooooowly, press the soles of their feet together and lazily caress each other with their tentacles. This gentle swaying foreplay can last for up to twenty hours. In some species, a special organ—a love dart made from calcium—is deployed. One of the two snails suddenly sticks this thin, hard dagger into the foot of the other snail. This arrow is a true sex weapon: a dagger with four blades, which ensures that the sperm cells survive and reach the egg. Sometimes the two snails stab each other, which means they can fertilize one other, becoming both father and mother at the same time.

DEADLY
Praying Mantises

With her front legs bent, the praying mantis always looks as though she is sending her prayers to heaven, but she doesn't behave so devoutly when she's procreating. The male approaches his partner very slowly and carefully from behind. Any careless movement could provoke a deadly attack. When he's close enough, the male jumps on the female's back and the hours-long mating can begin. Sometimes the male lives to hand over his seed package. In some species of mantis the female turns around and starts to eat her sperm donor. Even without a head the male mantis can complete the act of fertilization. Usually he ends up as a whole-body meal for the mother of descendants that he will unfortunately never get to know.

EVERYTHING UNDER CONTROL

SPOON TRICK
Damselflies

The male damselfly needs to be sure he's the one and only. He does this with his "spoon trick." He first uses his penis, not to transfer his sperm, but to clear the way, in case another male has been there before him. His penis has a kind of scoop at the front, with which he can remove the sperm of his predecessor from the female's abdomen before actually mating. Not even a tiny remnant should be left. Only when everything is spanking clean does the damselfly male proceed to fertilize the female.

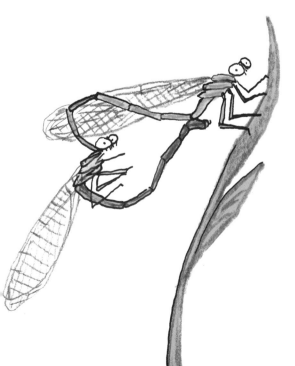

SCRAM!
Cabbage White Butterflies

These delicate white butterflies like to flutter through our gardens, especially vegetable gardens with cabbages. A male cabbage butterfly seems intent on being,

and remaining, the only partner for his mate. The others can push off! So during mating, he sprays the female with a very special perfume. From then on, she is no longer attractive to other males. To them, for some reason, she stinks!

RECLUSIVE
Moles

Male moles like to make sure that they're the father of any offspring. Immediately after mating, they seal the female's vaginal entrance with a sticky liquid. This extra contribution hardens into a plug and acts like a cork in a bottle. The sperm of any possible successors will have no chance of reaching the egg cells of the female mole, and the male can be sure that he is truly the father of the tiny blind moles that will soon be born. In addition, the mother and offspring are well protected by the plug from bacteria that could travel through the vaginal opening into the abdomen.

TAKING PRECAUTIONS
Chickens

A rooster in a henhouse has a lot to do because he usually lives with several hens. He has to keep the females together and defend them. Of course he usually fathers all the chicks, so the hens have to make sure they each receive enough sperm for their eggs since they greatly

outnumber him. They stock up, storing the rooster's sperm in the tiny niches of their Fallopian tubes where it can last for about two weeks and be given to the egg cells that ripen regularly. Then, within a day, a cell develops into a hard-shelled chicken egg that is laid in the nest. If a hen doesn't want an inexperienced rooster as the father of her chicks, she can simply eject his sperm and wait for a better candidate to come along.

Crab Spiders

When some species of crab spider mate, the female waits, ready and motionless, for the arrival of the much smaller male. She dangles from a thread or sits on a leaf. With quick movements he jumps on his spider woman and binds her to a leaf with his silk. Now he can crawl under her abdomen and calmly insert his sperm into her. The female can easily free herself after insemination, which makes the whole thing look more like a game than actual captivity.

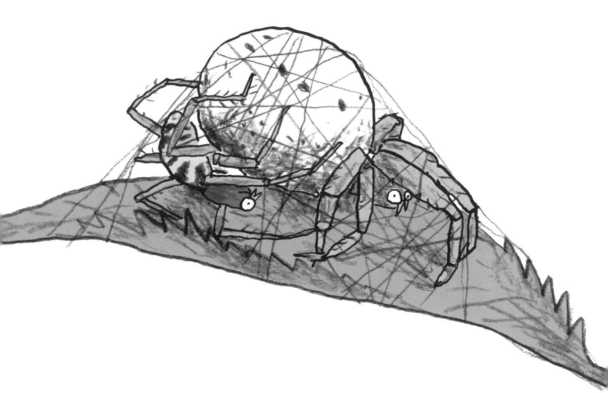

GIFTS, BRIBES AND PAYMENTS

EXCHANGE OF GOODS AND SERVICES
Adélie Penguins

These small Antarctic penguins build their nests from pebbles that they peck out of the ice or find on the beach. It's not so easy, though. There simply aren't enough stones. Many thousands of penguins breed at the same time and they all want to lay their eggs in well-built stone nests. Some female penguins collect the coveted stones by making a kind of deal with male penguins—sex in exchange for stones. A female will find the nest of a single male (a suitable distance away from her own nest) and climb in. After the male has mounted her, the female takes a pebble in payment and happily waddles back to her own nest and her own partner.

FOOD OF LOVE
Kingfishers

Small gifts can preserve a friendship or lead to one. A kingfisher impresses his chosen female by bringing her fish as a gift. He feeds her to demonstrate the care he'll give their brood later on. If the female is convinced (and full of fish), she will willingly mate with him.

BRIBERY
Scorpionflies

The male scorpionfly has to provide a lot to keep his female happy. He keeps dead insects or homemade spitballs on offer during the mating season. As long as the female is nibbling, the male can mate with her from behind. The equation is simple: the more gifts, the longer the pleasure. If the spitballs run out during the act of love, he'd better make some more, and fast. He'll only be allowed to mate as long as the female is kept fed.

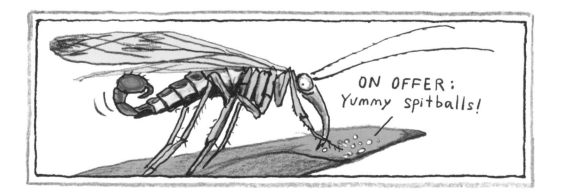

SEX FOR GROOMING
Macaques

Macaques are also prepared to "pay" for sex. A female is more likely to mate with a male who is friendly towards her, including grooming her to get the lice and fleas out of her fur. The length of the grooming session depends on the number of females in the area. If fewer females are available, the male must groom his partner longer to get sex. If, on the other hand, there are many females around, the price drops. Then the male has a lot less delousing to do.

BIRDS OF A FEATHER

There are many reasons why animals have sex.

★ **Mainly for reproduction.**

★ **Sometimes to help them live together peacefully.**

★ **Sometimes out of pure animal lust.**

★ **Sometimes to determine the hierarchy (ranking) of the group.**

★ **Sometimes for other reasons that aren't clear.**

With many species there is sex and affection between same-sex partners. Here are a few examples.

MALES WITH MALES
Dolphins

Adult male dolphins live in all-male pods, and male pairs can form lifelong bonds. You'll often see two males swimming side by side, fondling or stimulating each other with their snouts or penises, or looking after each other if one is sick or injured. When it comes time for reproduction, they'll search for a female to mate with. But after sex it's very clear that the female is no longer of interest, and that the stronger partnership is between the two males.

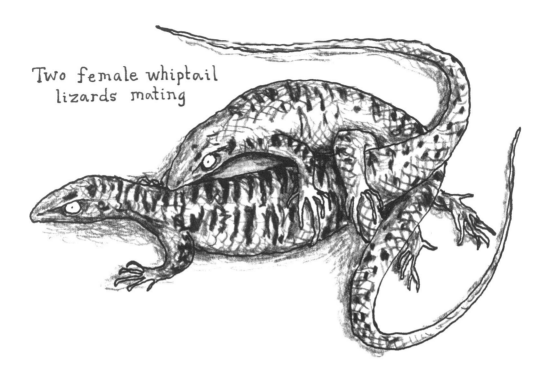

Two female whiptail lizards mating

UNNECESSARY MALES
Whiptail Lizards

Some species of whiptail lizard exist only as females. So a female can have offspring without being fertilized by sperm from a male. This is called parthenogenesis.

The mating looks exactly as it does with other reptiles, but what takes place is different because two females are lying on each other and pressing their sexual openings together. Only with this stimulus can the female on the bottom produce eggs. Of course, these eggs produce only female lizards, which will one day mate with females to produce female offspring...

Is it a girl or a girl?

FEMALE PAIRS
Roseate Terns

Some roseate terns also live happily in female pairs, even though males are available. Two females lay their eggs in a common nest and look after them

together. As with other bird pairs, one goes after food and the other stays home on the nest and takes care of the brood. In these cases, the males serve more or less as sperm donors, with whom the females engage only briefly. After mating, the female immediately returns to her female partner to raise the brood.

JOINT LEADERS

Lions

Sometimes two male lions live together as a couple. They play with each other, climb on each other and can also lead a pack together. Time and again, they demonstrate that they respect and are devoted to one another.

WHO'S THE BOSS?

Guinea Pigs

Male guinea pigs sometimes mount each other. They don't do it to produce children, because that wouldn't work. They do it to determine their ranking in the group. It's how guinea pig leaders show that they have the last word and that the others are subordinate. A group with a clear and undisputed hierarchy makes all the animals feel secure. And this order must be clarified from time to time, sometimes by same-sex mounting.

There are many animal species that behave sexually with others of the same sex:

giraffes, storks, elephants, penguins, bison, flamingos, vultures, elephant seals, deep-water octopuses, antelopes, orcas, fruit flies, parasitic wasps, cichlids, bonobos, sheep, damselflies, bedbugs, cows, ducks, zebras, birds of paradise, leopard seals, cranes, worms, greyling geese, macaques, woodpeckers, fallow deer, polecats, lizards, gorillas, weevils, koalas, albatrosses…

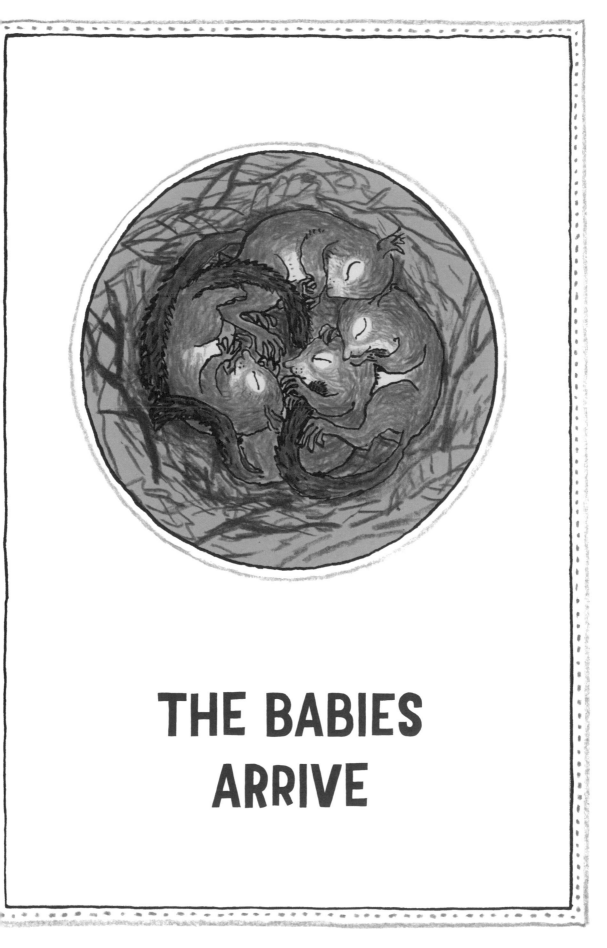

THE BABIES
ARRIVE

The beginning of life is especially dangerous for animal children, because most of them can't yet defend themselves against predators. Animals have evolved many different strategies to ensure the safety of their young—although some parents are distinctly careless!

With most **MAMMALS**, babies develop in the uterus and are born through the vagina. Once the baby is born, the mother licks it clean and often eats the umbilical cord and the placenta, which also come out of the vagina. This prevents predators from being attracted by the scent of the birth.

The father is often absent after the birth because in many species the mother raises the offspring. After all, she is the one who produces the milk to nourish the children. The young are often kept sheltered in a cave or nest at the beginning.

For most **BIRDS**, both parents are equally involved in incubating the eggs and raising the young. The chicks are blind at first. They don't have feathers to protect them and haven't yet learned how to fly.

The offspring of **FISH** and almost all **AMPHIBIANS**, **INSECTS**, **REPTILES** and **SPIDERS** are not so well off. Their eggs are often well guarded or stored in sheltered surroundings, but as soon as the offspring hatch, they're usually left to fend for themselves. The number of eggs is often extremely high to ensure that at least a few of them make it to adulthood.

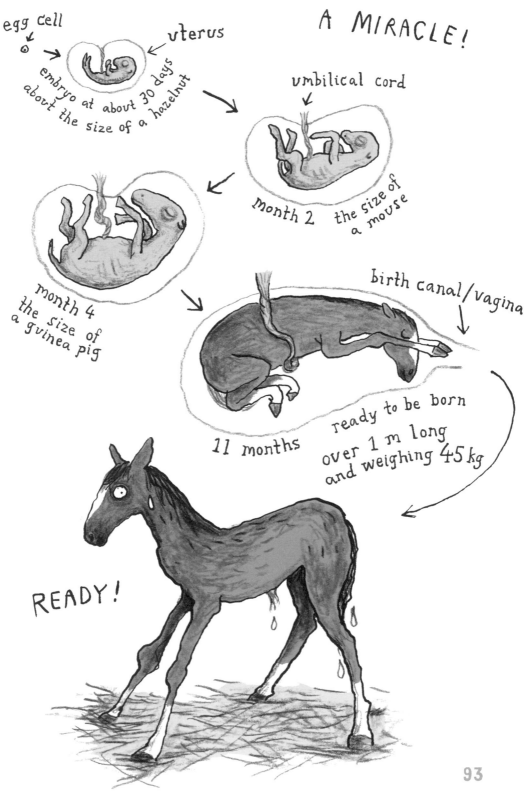

A fertilized egg cell turns into a baby

A MIRACLE!

egg cell

uterus

embryo at about 30 days
about the size of a hazelnut

umbilical cord

Month 2   the size of a mouse

month 4
the size of
a guinea pig

birth canal/vagina

11 months   ready to be born
over 1 m long
and weighing 45 kg

READY!

PREGNANCY

MISTER MAMA
Seahorses

When it comes to offspring, the male seahorse has a very special job. He's the one who hatches the eggs and takes care of the children. Once the female has deposited several hundred eggs into her partner's brood pouch, he fertilizes them with his sperm. The precious cargo grows in the safety of the father's pouch. Throughout the pregnancy, he stays in one place. With his tail wound around an aquatic plant, he waits for his partner's daily visits.

After a few weeks, the small seahorses hatch inside the thick pouch. The male has to strain and double over to squeeze the tiny beings out of his belly, much the way a mammal mother has contractions to give birth to her children.

EGG SURPRISE
Turtles

When turtle mothers lay their eggs, they consider carefully where to bury them. In many turtle species the sex of the offspring is not determined when the eggs are fertilized but according to the temperature of the environment. In a warmer environment, females will emerge from the eggs. But if the surrounding air is cooler, males will be born.

DOUBLE TROUBLE
European Brown Hares

Hares can have two pregnancies at the same time. How does this happen? Hares have sex often and a female brown hare may mate again while pregnant. With the uterus already occupied by growing embryos, the new embryos wait in the egg tubes. Once the first brood is born, the next embryos move into the uterus—and the mother hare must immediately prepare another nest for a second batch of siblings.

BIG MOUTH IN MORE WAYS THAN ONE

Darwin's Frogs

They have a funny name, they look weird, and their pregnancy is not the same as for other frogs. Normally, fertilized frog eggs are left to their fate. Tadpoles hatch and develop independently in the water into small frogs. But here's how it works with Darwin's frogs. The male patiently looks after the brood by taking the eggs into his mouth, where they hatch into tadpoles. The little ones stay well protected in the male's vocal sac and go on developing for about seven weeks. You can see in the frog's body the tumbling and jostling until at last it's "birth" day. The male frog opens his mouth, jerks briefly and spits out his developed frog children, one after another.

PREGNANT PAUSE
Roe Deer

Spring is a good time to be born. The weather is milder, plants are producing fresh leaves and it's easier to find food. Roe deer can make sure that their fawns are born at this easier time of year. The deer mother is already pregnant by high summer, and if her baby continued to develop normally, it would be born in the middle of the cold and barren winter, with a poor chance of survival. The roe deer can delay the pregnancy and keep the fertilized egg floating in the womb. The embryo develops later, to be born during the pleasanter days of spring.

★ ★ ★

PATIENT UNTIL BIRTH

Some animals born directly from their mother's uterus take years to grow ready to be born.
For others, it goes more quickly...

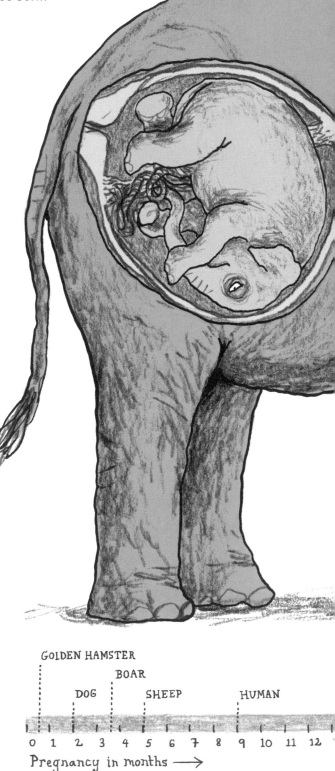

How long does it take before the baby is born?

GOLDEN HAMSTER

BOAR

DOG

SHEEP

HUMAN

0 1 2 3 4 5 6 7 8 9 10 11 12

Pregnancy in months ⟶

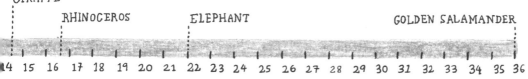

GIRAFFE

RHINOCEROS

ELEPHANT

GOLDEN SALAMANDER

14 15 16 17 18 19 20 21 22 23 24 25 26 27 28 29 30 31 32 33 34 35 36

ONE EGG IS THE SAME AS ALL THE OTHERS? SAYS WHO?

No matter how a living being comes into the world, most begin with an egg—a protective shell or first cell in which new life develops.

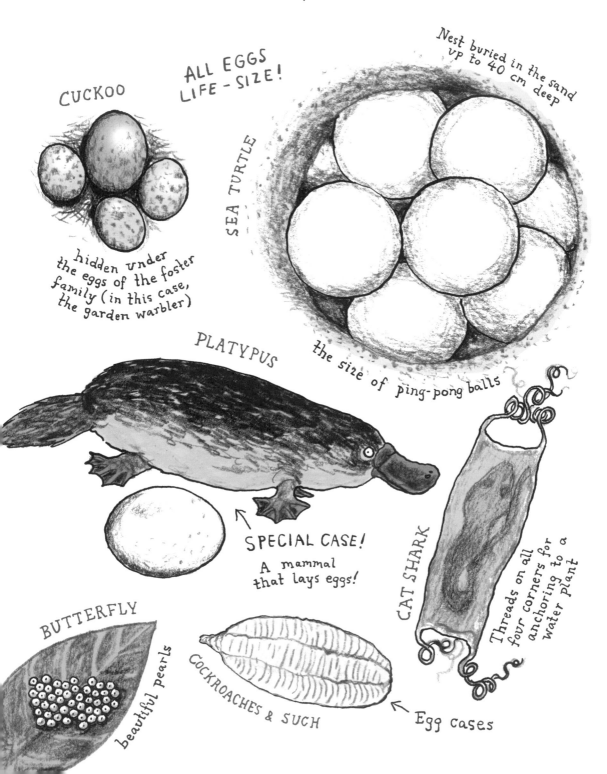

ALL EGGS LIFE-SIZE!

CUCKOO

hidden under the eggs of the foster family (in this case, the garden warbler)

SEA TURTLE

Nest buried in the sand up to 40 cm deep

the size of ping-pong balls

PLATYPUS

SPECIAL CASE!
A mammal that lays eggs!

CAT SHARK

Threads on all four corners for anchoring to a water plant

BUTTERFLY

beautiful pearls

COCKROACHES & SUCH

Egg cases

BEE HUMMINGBIRD   RECORD!

THE SMALLEST
BIRD'S EGG

BIGGEST EGG
OF ALL
(among living animals)

OSTRICH

life-size

Chickens with red
earlobes usually
lay brown eggs

egg cell → · HUMANS
have the largest body cells

Chickens with white
earlobes usually lay
white eggs

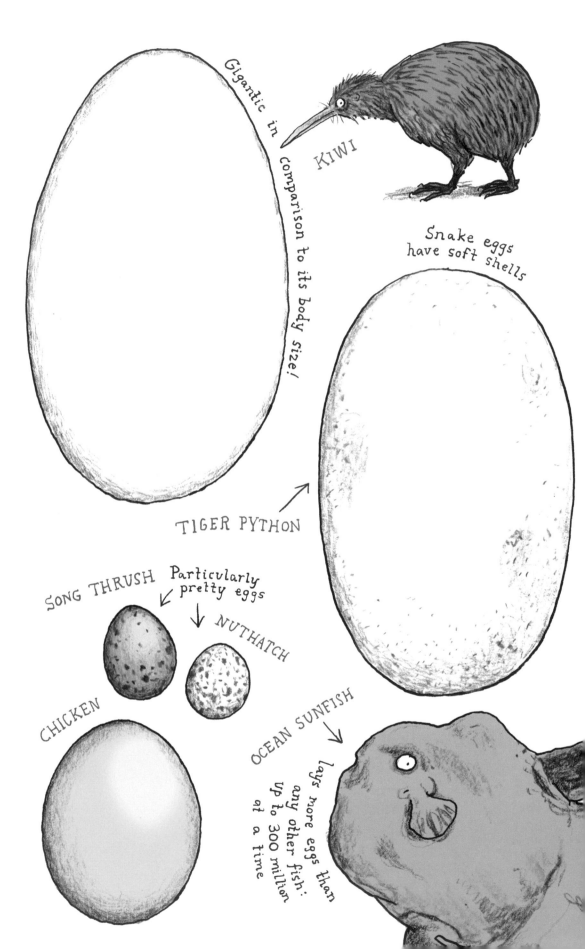

Gigantic in comparison to its body size!

KIWI

Snake eggs have soft shells

TIGER PYTHON

SONG THRUSH Particularly pretty eggs

NUTHATCH

CHICKEN

OCEAN SUNFISH

lays more eggs than any other fish: up to 300 million at a time

COMING INTO THE WORLD

BORN AGAIN
Kangaroos

When kangaroos are born, they're teeny-tiny and look more like shrivelled pinkish worms than hairy leaping marsupials. The tiny little something weighs about a gram when it's squeezed out of its mother's vagina. Naked, blind and deaf, it clings to its mother's fur and sets out on an exhausting journey. While the mother is still busy licking up the amniotic fluid and mucus, the baby—still only the size of a jelly bean—hauls itself up her belly and into the pouch. Within minutes the first lap of the journey is done. Deep down in the pouch are teats to suck on. There the tiny premature baby goes on developing, protected and left in peace. In the coming weeks and months, it will drink there, sleep, drink, grow, drink, pee, drink, grow fur, drink, develop sight and hearing, drink...and gradually it will turn into a real baby kangaroo, known as a joey.

Kangaroo baby when it is born the first time (original size)

Kangaroo baby born a second time

After about eight months it finally leaves the pouch — it is born a second time. It slides out into the world from the protection of its mother's belly and is soon able to bounce around pretty well on its hind legs.

For a year or so the kangaroo baby will climb back into its mother's pouch again and again, whenever it is frightened or needs protection. Later, even when it's too big to slip into the pouch, it can still stick its head in to drink milk from its mother's teats.

LONG WAY DOWN
Giraffes

Giraffes in the wild must always be alert for attacks by predators. Their strategy is to flee. That's why they mostly sleep standing up. Even when giving birth, a giraffe cow stays on her feet. From a height of two meters, the newborn simply falls to the ground. Fortunately, its bones are still very soft, so there's no harm done. After a few hours the baby giraffe can walk on its spindly legs and follow its mother's every step.

UPSIDE DOWN WITH A SAFETY NET
Bats

Bats don't only hang from their feet to sleep. They also give birth upside down. Working against gravity, but with the help of contractions, the hanging bat mother pushes the baby out of her vagina. She holds out her wings as a kind of safety net for the newborn. Fortunately from the moment they're born, little bat babies cling onto their mother by their feet. They immediately receive milk from her teats, and in a couple of weeks they can fly around just like the adults.

FIRST TOOTH
Chickens

Before it hatches, the chick in the egg grows a little tooth on its beak. When it's time to hatch, the chick makes the first hole from inside the shell, using the tooth like the tip of a pick. Then it has a brief rest while it breathes air for the first time. The chick then wriggles and wrestles against the hard eggshell until, with incredible force, it breaks open a larger hole to hatch out of. Now it can rest for a while! In a few hours, it will greet its siblings and mother as a fluffy chick. It no longer needs the egg tooth, which simply disappears or falls off after a few days.

The chicken siblings "arrange" to hatch together. A few days before the hard work of birth they communicate through their eggshells with loud cheeping. When the time comes, they start to use their egg teeth almost simultaneously, each one working to set itself free.

Midget Livebearers

In this species of fish, the young hatch from their eggs inside the mother's belly before being born into the water. As their name suggests, these fish are very, very tiny, so the female doesn't have much room available for her children to grow inside her. The eggs mature one at a time so that younger babies have time to grow while their older siblings are being born. At this rate, it can take several weeks for up to 40 midget fish to be born.

BREECH BIRTH
Dolphins

Unlike other mammals, dolphins are born tail first, so they can go on receiving enough oxygen through the umbilical cord. If they came out head first the way most humans do, the young would be in danger of suffocating at birth. Immediately after a baby is born, it instinctively swims to the surface to breathe on its own—often guided by the mother or another female. The mother is not alone during the birth. The entire dolphin community is often there to help.

MOTHERS AND FATHERS

PIGGYBACK
Giant Waterbugs

When some species of giant waterbug are expecting offspring, the fathers take all responsibility for them. After her eggs are fertilized, the female bug sticks them onto the father's back with a special glue. The father carries this load of more than a hundred eggs. As he moves, sleeps and searches for food, his developing children are always with him. When he goes swimming, he must be extra careful not to drown them (they need air).

The female goes on her way, knowing that her offspring will be well cared for.

Once the babies have hatched, you can sometimes see the waterbug father with a bit of eggshell still stuck to his back. How free and light he must feel with the children finally off his back!

SELF-SACRIFICING
Octopuses

As soon as small octopuses hatch from their eggs, they're on their own. They have no idea how much their mother has sacrificed to get them this far! A female octopus gets only one chance at

motherhood. She guards more than a hundred eggs day and night, spreading her body protectively over her brood and fanning water over them again and again to ensure they develop well. During this time she barely eats.

Over time (guarding and caring for the eggs can take two to 10 months), she grows paler and thinner. Once the mother octopus has done her job and the little octopuses have hatched, she dies of exhaustion and starvation.

PARENTING THREESOME

Hedge Sparrows

Although these brownish-gray birds are nondescript, they don't hold back when choosing a mate, and the female occasionally pairs with two different males. Before mating, a male will often peck at the female's cloaca to try and remove a rival male's sperm. Each male thinks that he's the father and they both

throw themselves into looking after the brooding female, bringing a good supply of nutritious worms and protecting the nest from enemies. Meanwhile, the female can stay put, knowing she and her brood will be well looked after.

LOVING CANNIBALS
Siamese Fighting Fish

With their brilliant feathery fins, these fish look as beautiful as birds of paradise. But Siamese fighting fish can be quite aggressive, biting and shoving their mating rivals until one of them dies.

The single male that's left turns out to be a caring father. He uses his spit to make air bubbles and works hard to build a soft, foamy nest on the surface of the water. After a combative courtship dance, he mates with the female beneath the nest, where she lays her eggs. Now the father carefully collects the fertilized eggs in his mouth and spits them into the beautiful nest. He checks constantly to make sure the nest and eggs are doing well. Sleep is out of the question. He's too busy returning eggs to the nest, maintaining it and protecting the brood from enemies.

But watch out! Once the little ones hatch and swim, they'd better get out of there fast, because the father is no longer interested in running a nursery. He has a taste for little Siamese fighting fish.

A MILLION DESCENDANTS
Fruit Flies

Fruit flies are everywhere—on rotting pieces of fruit, in raisin bread or in unwashed juice glasses. In summer, once the tiny, yellow-brown, red-eyed creatures have settled in the kitchen, they multiply in no time, swirling around fruit baskets by the hundreds. A female fly can lay up to 400 mini-eggs in her lifetime. Barely visible to the naked eye, larvae soon emerge from the eggs and are well supplied with food by all the juicy peaches, spotty apples and rotting apricots in which they were born. Many have only a short life, however, for most fruit fly larvae slip unseen into the tummies of fruit eaters.

Once the larvae are fully grown fruit flies, the females can mate and lay new eggs at the tender age of 10 hours. A single pair of fruit flies can therefore produce millions of children, grandchildren and great-grandchildren within a month.

WORKSHARING
Emperor Penguins

In the freezing temperatures and icy winds of Antarctica, emperor penguins take on a lot for the sake of their brood. The father is the one who is mainly in charge of hatching the single egg. In

an act of pure devotion, he places it on his feet and covers it with his warm belly-fold (brood pouch). Over the next few weeks, he'll take care of it on his own while the female heads out to sea to find food. Happily, the male shares a smart community with the many other left-behind fathers, which makes it easier to withstand the wind and weather. All the penguins move close together to keep each other warm in the extreme cold. They keep things fair, too, so that everyone takes turns standing in the cozy middle or shivering on the icy edges. During this time, they eat nothing and lose a lot of weight. They quench their thirst with snow. It takes about two months for the eggs to hatch. Then the father's belly-fold provides a warm shelter where the chick is lovingly fed with "daddy's milk" from the hungry father's stomach.

Soon the mothers return from the sea full of fish. Each can recognize her partner from the hundreds of look-alikes by his special call. At last he is off duty and free to feed and regain his strength. Now the parents take turns caring for their young. By next breeding season, they will have had lots of practice for raising a sibling.

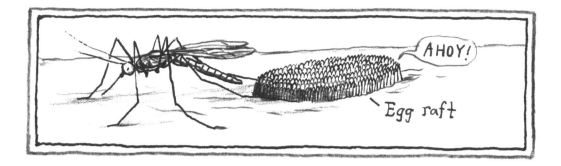

Egg raft

EVERYTHING FOR THE KIDS
Mosquitoes

When it comes time to mate, the males of some species of mosquito form a dense swarm into which the female can fly to be fertilized. The female then becomes thirsty for blood, which she needs to produce her eggs. No blood, no mosquito babies. So she goes in search of an animal or human whose blood she can suck through her proboscis. A day or two after she has pumped the host's protein-rich blood into her body, she lays her eggs, all together in a kind of raft on the surface of standing water.

Perhaps the next time you scratch a mosquito bite, it will help to know that the mosquito mother is simply caring for her offspring.

By the way, the male mosquitoes don't bite. They prefer plant juices as food.

ABSOLUTE RULE OF THE FAT QUEEN
Termites

In the middle of a termite community is the single queen and her partner. The entire colony of millions revolves around her. All the work, building and activity is for her well-being. The termite mound is like a palace for the royal couple, built high off the ground with underground tunnels, air ducts and chambers. The main thing is to keep it nice and cool so the two rulers can pursue their only

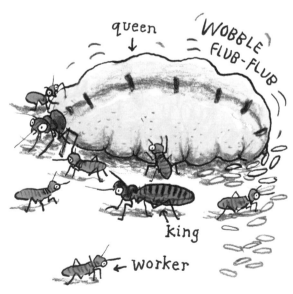

queen

WOBBLE FLUB-FLUB

king

← worker

pastimes—sex and egg-laying. At some point, the queen is so fat that she's like a bloated egg machine, pushing out one fertilized egg every three seconds—about 30,000 a day.

All one or two million termites in a mound are the children of a single mother and father. Maybe that's why they all look alike.

MAMA'S BOY

Bonobos

Bonobo children are extremely attached to their mother. In the first years of life, they constantly cling to her belly or back and drink from her teats.

For many years, they sleep near their mother and let themselves be carried around by her, even long after they're independent. She passes on the rules of survival: how to behave in the group, knowledge about plants and enemies, and how to make their way through dense jungle. Bonobo mothers also play intensively with their children and care for them round the clock, especially their sons.

The male's relationship with his mother lasts his entire life. Even when he's grown and looking for his own mating partner, his mother is by his side. She acts as go-between with the females and, if necessary, intervenes in confrontations with other males.

DIFFICULT BIRTHS

SAVAGE SIBLINGS

Sand Tiger Sharks

During pregnancy, real carnage takes place in the belly of a sand tiger shark mother. Initially, 20 to 40 fertilized eggs rest in the two wombs, each egg containing a tiny developing shark. It's clear there won't be room for everyone! After about four months, the embryos in the mother's wombs hatch from their eggs. They're about as big as a child's hand at this point, and their jaws are fully developed. The feast can begin.

Over time, the strongest (usually the first to hatch) eat their weaker and less-developed siblings as well as all the unfertilized eggs still in the womb. They need this food to grow. After a couple of months, two strong, well-nourished and well-developed shark babies are born, one from each uterus. Even in the womb they've used the rule that will define their lives as predators: eat or be eaten.

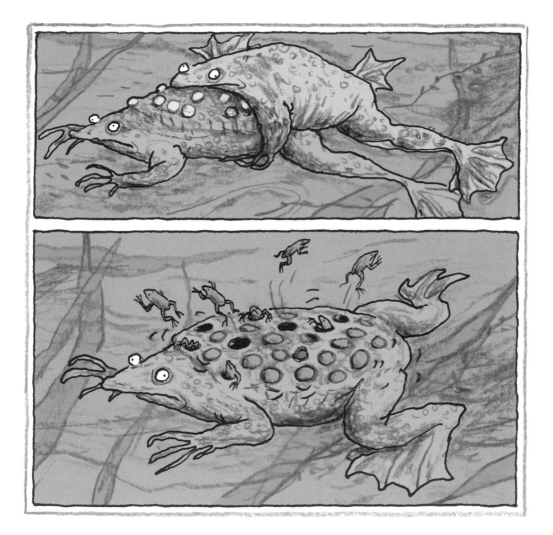

PREGNANT HOLES
Surinam Toads

Somersaults in the water. That's what Surinam toads do in pairs, one after another, until they get completely dizzy. As they cling together, the female releases egg after egg while the male simultaneously fertilizes them. Then the male lies on the female and presses the 100 or so fertilized eggs firmly into her back. Her plump body is now adorned with many small white beads. Her spongy skin grows around the eggs until they've sunk below the surface. There they're incubated. After a few months, things get uneasy under the mother's skin. Here and there, then over her entire back, the skin breaks as arms, legs and finally entire baby toads emerge into the open. A movie about aliens has nothing on this! What's left is a scarred mother toad, whose skin will take time to heal and regrow.

NOT FOR THE TIMID
Parasitic Mites

Right before giving birth, the belly of the mother in this mite species looks like a huge ball. Her eggs ripen in her body, where the larvae also hatch and pupate. Now the mite children only have to be born from her bloated abdomen. But what awaits the mother is like a scene from a horror movie. At first, all the male mites hatch. No sooner have they seen the light of day than they rush back to their mother, pierce her body and suck out all her fluids. Fattened and strengthened, they wait for their sisters to be born. When the females' birth begins, the males pull them by the hind legs from their dying mother's body and mate with them on the spot. The poor things! They've barely made it into the world and now they face the same fate as their mother.

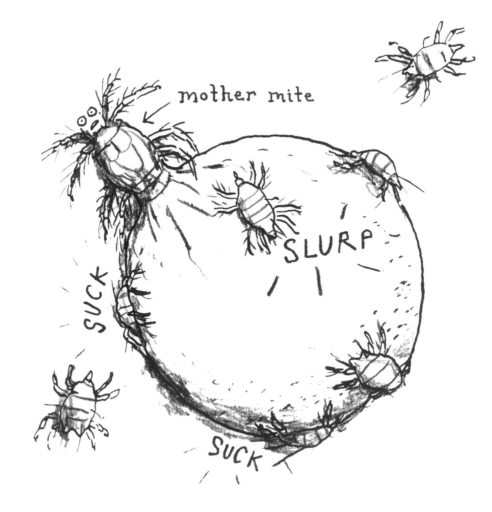

mother mite

SLURP

SUCK

SUCK

PREGNANT IN A FOREIGN BODY

Jewel Wasps

Jewel wasps impress with their dazzling appearance. But the way they reproduce is not at all pretty. The female needs another creature, usually a common cockroach, to host her eggs. She attacks it and, after a quick fight, stuns it with a poisonous sting into its brain. To completely disorient her defenceless victim, she also bites off its antennae. Then she drags the sedated cockroach into a small burrow, lays one of her eggs in it and seals the burrow as quickly as she can with small stones. The cockroach is now walled in alive and, for the short remainder of its life, serves as surrogate mother and food source for the jewel wasp's larva. The hungry wasp child eats the cockroach's innards and transforms inside its body into a new, iridescent jewel wasp.

★ ★ ★

TEATS AND UDDERS

Mammals drink their mother's milk after birth. This supplies them with the vital nutrients they need for growing up.

The teats or mammary glands, like breasts on humans, always come as a pair. A mother has on average twice as many teats as the number of children she gives birth to at a time.

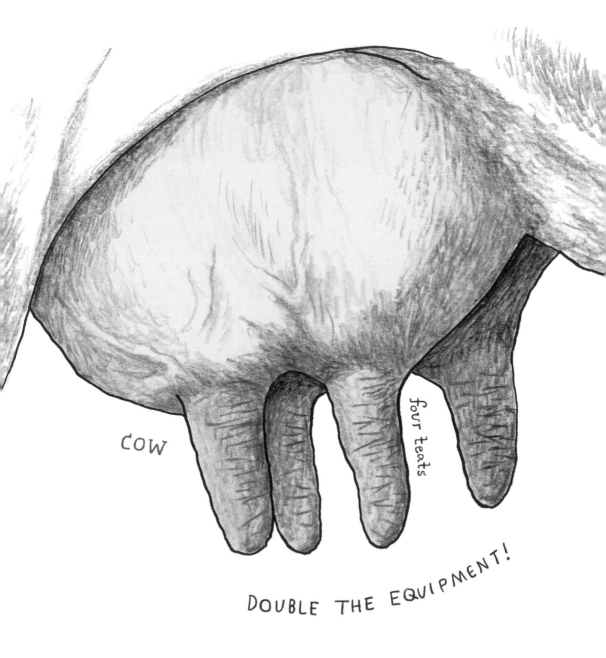

COW

four teats

DOUBLE THE EQUIPMENT!

A CHILD'S LIFE

Sloths

This animal lives life in slow motion. It's quite a while before small sloths can hang from branches and eat leaves on their own. Once born, they cling fast to their mother and don't leave her soft,-furry belly for five or six months. From the safety of the mother-hammock they learn skills for later life: how to pick and eat leaves, how to move from one tree to another, and various climbing tricks. All of this is done in a very calm, leisurely way.

RESIGNED TO FATE
Green Spoon Worms

When the larvae of these sea worms first hatch from their eggs, they have no definitive sex. Life starts as a game of chance, with their future determined by where the water currents take them. If they land on the sandy seabed, they develop into female worms. But if a larva lands on a female worm, it becomes a tiny male and is soon swallowed by the female. For the rest of its days, it will remain inside the genitals of the female, where, along with many

I'm staying here.

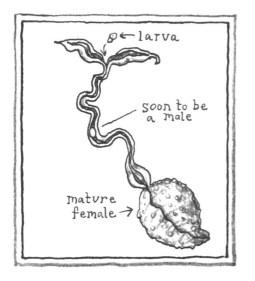

larva

soon to be
a male

mature
female →

constantly come to the surface for air.

This is why young sea turtles don't hatch from their eggs at sea. A sea turtle mother always returns to the beach where she herself was born. She lays her eggs there in the sand to be incubated by the sun's warmth.

When the time comes, the little ones peel themselves from their eggs with huge effort and dig their way out of the sand. However, the biggest challenge of their young lives lies ahead. Along with thousands of siblings simultaneously hatched, they must cross the hot sand to reach their actual habitat, the sea. They paddle awkwardly towards the water. No mother or grownup turtle is nearby to protect them on their dangerous journey. Above and around them, seabirds and other hungry predators are waiting to fight over a meal of tender young turtle. Only a few reach the cool sea where they can finally feel safer.

other swallowed males, it has only one important job: to fertilize the eggs of the female with its seed. So, should you ever meet a green spoon worm, you can bet that it's a female.

ON THEIR OWN
Sea Turtles

Sea turtles are unbelievably good divers and swimmers. They can cover huge distances underwater. And yet they must

So, what shall we play now?

SURPRISINGLY GOOD PARENTS
Ravens

Blind and naked raven chicks remain dependent on their parents for a long time after hatching. The nestlings are lovingly supplied with worms, insects and fruits until they're big enough to leave the nest. Still, these fledglings can't yet fly properly. When they sit looking helpless on the ground or tree branches, it might seem that the raven parents have pushed them from the nest and left them to fend for themselves. But that's not the case at all! The mother and father raven are always nearby. They continue to feed their offspring on the ground and defend them against enemies until the babies finally learn to fly. These very clever birds also like to play with their children. They might roll down snow hills, dangle upside down from branches or throw nuts to each other like balls.

BACKPACK
Scorpions

A scorpion mother is easy to recognize because she carries her kids around with her all the time. After hatching, the white mini-scorpions crawl onto their mother's back and stay there for a few weeks in a teeming swarm. The mother fearlessly protects her young from enemies with her venomous stinger, and she provides them with fluid through her skin. Soon the little scorpions are strong enough to leave their mother's back and tackle life on their own.

of breast milk. Sometimes a newborn sibling is already in there, sucking on one of the teats. The kangaroo mother is now a milk bar for two, providing the right type of milk from each teat. The little baby gets fat-rich milk because it still has a lot of growing to do. The bigger sibling drinks a lighter version because it has moved on to mainly solid food.

THE MILK BAR
Kangaroos

After about six months, a kangaroo baby is big enough to leave his mother's protective pouch. Grasses and leaves are now on the menu. But the young kangaroo keeps hopping back to his mother to stick his head in her pouch for a shot

DAYCARE
Greylag Geese

Greylag geese help each other out. Often there are "daycares" in the colony, where the goslings are brought while their parents go looking for food. Other greylag goose mothers supervise the young geese and make sure nothing happens to them.

SPRING AWAKENING
Polar Bears

Unlike most animals, polar bears give birth in winter. The female protects and hides her children, spending the first months with them inside a deep snow cave. Polar bear cubs are tiny and blind at birth, and barely have any fur. They weigh about as much as a pound of butter. In the early days, the cubs (there are usually two) depend entirely on their mother's nutritious milk and care. They stay snug in the snow den for about four months. Luckily, the mother has eaten enough during the summer months to put on a layer of fat so she can live without food during this time.

In spring, the cubs are big enough to stretch their paws out of the den for the first time. They're curious and playful as they set out to explore their surroundings. Their mother is always nearby to guard and play with her boisterous bear children. With her they'll always find protection and learn vital polar bear lessons in running, swimming, diving and hunting.

FAMILY LIFE

Ostriches

Females (hens) have an easy life in the ostrich herd because they barely have to worry about childcare. That job belongs mainly to the male ostrich that dominates the herd. He prepares the hollow where the eggs are to be hatched. Then the mating season begins, when the male mounts several hens. All the fertilized eggs go into the communal nest. Within two weeks, there can be up to 40 eggs from different mothers, and often different fathers (ostriches aren't too fussy).

The first hen to mate with the head male becomes his main mate. The other females he mates with don't take responsibility for the babies, though they still belong to the family. Over the coming weeks the ostrich male takes charge of the offspring, including the care and protection of all the eggs. His hen partner helps and relieves him from time to time. They're both the proud parents of a sizeable brood, although no one can say exactly who has which mother or father. It doesn't matter. The main thing is that the family stays together!

EXTENDED FAMILY
Meerkats

Meerkats live as a large cooperative family in an underground system of passageways. All the community tasks are clearly assigned. There are guards who watch over the construction of the burrow and keep an eye out for enemies by standing on their hind legs and scanning their surroundings. At the first sign of danger, they warn the others with a shrill squeak: Everyone get back home! The nannies look after the offspring. They keep the tiny meerkat babies warm and watch over the older children. Some meerkats provide food for everyone.

Young meerkats learn early from experienced adults how to hunt for beetles and dangerous scorpions. Just like school students, they must try again and again until they're skilled enough to bite the venomous stinger from a live scorpion, so it can't hurt them.

One female is the boss of all the family members. She decides where the entire clan goes. If any other females give birth, their babies are killed. That's how she keeps control of the whole extended family.

ALL SET FOR A FAMILY PHOTO!

FEMALE FAMILY TIES
African Elephants

Strong women stick together. This is a golden rule that elephants follow their entire lives. A herd is almost always led by an experienced cow who makes sure that all the children are properly raised and that valuable experience is shared with all the members of the group. She remains the leader of the herd until the end of her life. With her incredible elephant memory, she remembers important feeding sites and decades-old routes to water sources. She's the one who sets off first when the herd is on the move. When there's danger, she gathers everyone together in a tight group and makes sure the youngest are safely in the middle.

Female solidarity also kicks in if an animal is sick or injured. A weak herd member is looked after by the entire family group.

Sisters or aunts take on the role of midwives who support an elephant cow giving birth. Males (bulls) leave the herd once they reach puberty, often joining an all-male herd. They will join a female herd again only briefly, in order to mate.

127

SOCIETY OF CARING MOTHERS
Wild Boars

Wild boar herds (called "sounders") consist almost entirely of females and their many children. Sows and piglets range over their territory in a large family group. The oldest and most experienced sow is the leader. Male animals (hogs) are only tolerated in the community for mating. Otherwise they roam the forests as lone bachelors.

When offspring are born in spring, each sow is responsible for the welfare of her litter. She builds a nest padded with grass and leaves to protect the sensitive newborns from cold and damp. Soon the sows form nursing communities, often lying as a group on the forest floor while the greedy piglets suckle.

Sometimes one of the young mistakenly nurses from the wrong mother. Fortunately, the clever forest animals have a good sense of smell so the oversight is quickly sniffed out and the little wanderer sent back to its real mother. Over time, each piglet settles on its own preferred teat, defending it against its many hungry, jostling siblings.

Head Hyena

FEMALE COMMANDO
Spotted Hyenas

A herd of spotted hyenas is loud and aggressive, always fighting, biting and arguing. Interestingly, the attack leaders of the pack are female, and they keep the clan together. Even the most powerful male has to submit to all the females. After a communal hunt, the spoils are divided strictly according to rank. The female leader with her children claims the right to eat her fill. Then the other females have their turn and finally there may be something left for the males.

MACHO MALE
Sacred Baboons

In this species, one male baboon is the absolute boss of up to 10 females. He alone decides where they go, which of his females may pick the lice out of his coat, or which gets to mate with him. And woe to the females who don't like it! They're threatened with beatings and bloody bites from the boss. It can also happen that several leaders share or swap females among themselves.

If the leader becomes too old or weak, or dies, a new one takes over and demolishes the old order. All the children of the former leader are killed and the females are expected to produce new offspring with the new boss. And it's probably not hard to guess which of the two parents has to raise and take care of the babies once they're born.

Boss Baboon

RELUCTANT FOSTER PARENTS
Cuckoos

It can be exhausting and tedious, feeding, raising and caring for children. That's why the cuckoo has developed a particular tactic: let others do the work! This does take planning, however. The female cuckoo looks for the finished nest of another bird species and spies on the breeding pair who use it. At the right moment, she lays her own egg beside those already in the nest, eating or tossing out one of the eggs already there so the number stays the same. Amazingly, the cuckoo's egg looks almost the same as those of the host family. So the nest's owners don't recognize it as a foreign egg and simply treat it as their own.

Born blind and naked, the cuckoo hatchling is visibly bigger than its siblings. At once, the newborn exerts all its force to shove any other eggs or freshly hatched chicks out of the nest. The bird parents seem to notice none of this. The cuckoo kid screams loudly with its orange beak, demanding that they feed it at once.

Like an overinflated feather ball, the fat foster child is now in a nest too small for it. Nevertheless, it will be lovingly raised over the next weeks and constantly supplied with insects. Soon it will be many times bigger than its daintier parents.

130

ADOPTION
Chimpanzees

Time and time again, animals that live in a group will care for the offspring of sick or dead members of their species to ensure their protection. When a baby chimpanzee's mother dies, the child is often adopted by another member of its family or wider group, lovingly cared for and protected from danger. Without this support, it would surely not survive.

ADOPTION II
Lions

It's astonishing, but in rare cases a kind of adoption occurs between different animal species with completely different roles. In Kenya, for example, there was a lioness who "adopted" several baby antelopes. She was particularly aggressive in defending her adopted babies from other lions. They must have been very surprised to see a delicious meal protected with such devotion.

SHARED ACCOMMODATION

Sociable Weaver Birds

These South African birds live in huge community nests—tree dwellings that have often existed for decades. They're constantly improved, renovated and expanded by generations of birds, so that sometimes a hundred pairs of sociable weavers nest there at the same time. All live under one roof and are well protected from temperature changes, rain and enemies. Work is constantly being carried out as the individual sleeping and brood chambers are rewoven and repaired.

Sometimes the branch on which a giant nest hangs can no longer bear the weight. Then the whole palatial construction crashes to the ground and a new years-long team project begins for the weaver birds.

SINGLE PARENT

Brown Bears

The bear father puts his feet up long before the birth of his children. It's the mother who raises and feeds the young, aggressively defending them against other predators. When danger threatens, she scares the cubs up a tree and bravely faces the enemy alone. Above all, she takes care that no strange male bear comes near. He would kill the young bears in order to mate with her.

In their first years together, the cubs learn all the vital life skills from their mother. She patiently shows them how to get honey, where to catch the best fish and how fast they must run to escape danger. After two to three years, the mother bear knows that her children can manage on their own. For her, it's time to mate with a new partner and produce

more offspring. Again and again she drives the young bears away with loud growls, paw swipes and warning bites, signalling that it's time for them to fend for themselves.

Black Swans

Now and then two male black swans live together as a couple. Sometimes they even have eggs in their nest, which they care for together. Of course, the eggs come from a female swan because only she can lay them. Either the males have stolen them from another nest, or they've chased away the female, or she has abandoned her nest. At any rate, the two males do just as good a job at hatching the eggs.

Incidentally, the chicks that grow up with two fathers do particularly well. They have a much greater chance of survival than those growing up with a father and a mother. Because the males of this species are much larger than the females, they can behave more aggressively as a couple, asserting themselves over others and searching over a larger territory for food.

LIFELONG DEVOTION

Beavers

Only rarely do animals seek a partner for life and stay together forever. Once beavers have chosen a mate, they are truly faithful. They live with their families in dens and dams made from plant material, which they constantly rebuild and repair. When the older children leave, the next generation moves up. If a beaver parent dies, the other parent soon searches for a new partner so they can start a new family and hopefully remain together forever.

Just love hanging around on my own.

Orangutans

Not all mammals live together in groups or families. Some prefer to roam alone and at most find a member of the same species to mate with for a couple of hours. Orangutans are such loners. Orangutan means "man of the forest." These apes traverse their rainforest habitat using their long arms and legs to climb and wander. They know their way around. They know which trees have ripe fruit and where best to build sleeping nests for the night. Hearing another orangutan nearby, they howl to warn off the stranger. The peace-loving animals prefer to keep to themselves and shy away from conflicts with their own species. Family groups form only between females and their children, who roam through the large forests together.

ANIMAL BABIES

OPOSSUM
very resilient →

BEAR

at birth no
bigger than a
guinea pig

↑
one month old

ORANGUTAN

breastfed for
up to eight years →

HIPPOPOTAMUS

nice and fat
↓

must take a deep breath
to drink from the mother's
udder under water

OTTER
excellent water mattress →

CROCODILE

after they hatch, the mother carries her children gently into the water

piggyback

KOALA

SQUIRREL

teeny-tiny, but already sporting the giant paws it will need for climbing

SWAN

Mama boat ↓

RECORD
second among mammals

TENREC
32 Babies!

WHEW

GRAY SEAL
nurses five times a
day so it will grow three
times bigger on its
mother's fatty milk

INDEX OF ANIMALS

KATHARINA VON DER GATHEN

is a writer and sexuality educator. With Anke Kuhl, she published the book *Tell Me!*, which answers children's questions about sexuality, pregnancy and childbirth. The many questions children asked in her workshops about the sex lives of animals inspired her to write this book.

ANKE KUHL

is one of Germany's leading illustrators. She has illustrated more than 70 children's picture books and non-fiction books and has received a number of awards, including the German Youth Literature Prize.